HAITI PRIORITIZES:
COSTS AND BENEFITS FOR DEVELOPMENT SOLUTIONS

The Copenhagen Consensus Center is a think tank that researches and publishes the smartest solutions to the world's biggest problems. Our studies are conducted by more than 300 economists from internationally renowned institutions, including seven Nobel Laureates, to advise policymakers and philanthropists how to achieve the best results with their limited resources. The Center was voted Think Tank of the Year in International Affairs (US) by Prospect Magazine, and our advocacy for data-driven prioritization has been repeatedly voted one of the top 20 campaigns worldwide in a think tank survey conducted by the University of Pennsylvania.

The Haiti Priorise project talked to more than 700 people across Haiti to identify the best ways to help, and used radio, TV, and newspapers to spark a national conversation on the smartest solutions to the most pressing challenges. We engaged with more than 50 of the leading economists and sector experts in Haiti and around the world to estimate costs and benefits for 85 solutions, producing 1,000+ pages of new cost-benefit analysis research. Together with Nobel Laureate Vernon Smith and prominent Haitian economists Kesner Pharel, Raymond Magloire, and Ketleen Florestal we proposed the smartest ways to help Haiti move toward a more prosperous future.

For more information on our Haiti Priorise project, including the content of this book, please visit *haitipriorise.com* or contact Gaelle Prophete at *gaelle@copenhagenconsensus.com*.

HAITI PRIORITIZES:
COSTS AND BENEFITS
FOR DEVELOPMENT
SOLUTIONS

BY

BJORN LOMBORG & GAELLE PROPHETE

Copenhagen Consensus Center USA, Inc.

info@copenhagenconsensus.com
www.copenhagenconsensus.com

Copyright © 2018 by Copenhagen Consensus Center
Cover design by Rick Szuecs Design rickszuecs.com

This work was produced as part of the Haiti Priorise project.
This project was undertaken with the financial support of the Government of Canada. The opinions and interpretations in this publication are those of the authors and do not necessarily reflect those of the Government of Canada.

Canada

ISBN: 978-1-940003-19-1

CONTENTS

Eminent Panel Prioritization

About the Authors

Dr. Bjorn Lomborg is president of the Copenhagen Consensus Center and visiting professor at Copenhagen Business School. The Copenhagen Consensus Center is a think-tank that researches the smartest ways to do good. For this work, Lomborg was named one of TIME magazine's 100 most influential people in the world. His numerous books include "The Skeptical Environmentalist", "Cool It", "How to Spend $75 Billion to Make the World a Better Place" and "The Nobel Laureates' Guide to the Smartest Targets for the World 2016-2030." In 2016, Prospect Magazine awarded Copenhagen Consensus Center, US International Affairs Think Tank of the Year.

Gaelle Prophete is Director of Development for Copenhagen Consensus and Project Manager for *Haiti Priorise*. Her work spans public, private and international organizations across a variety of sectors.

ACADEMIC RESEARCHERS

Thank you to all of the researchers and collaborators who worked with us to make Haiti Priorise a major success.

Abbie Turiansky	Jean Edouard Pauyo	Rachel Sanders
Amien Sauveur	Jean Guy Honoré	Rachel Sklar
Anastasia Gage	Jeff Allien	Reina Engle-Stone
Anke Hoeffler	Jimmy Verne	Riphard Serent
Atonu Rabbani	Juan Belt	Romy Reggiani Theodat
Bahman Kashi	Karin Stenberg	Rudy Joseph
Bertrand Joseph	Katherine P. Adams	Ruolz Ariste
Bjorn Larsen	Ludovic Queuille	Ruth Christina Daurisca
Brian Hutchinson	Magdine Flore Rozier Baldé	Ryan K. McBain
Charley George Granvorka	Marc Jeuland	Samuel Philip Jean-Louis
Christine P. Stewart	Marcus Cadet	Stanley Jean-Baptiste
Dale Whittington	Mark Radin	Stephen A. Vosti
Damien Échevin	Mélissa Torchenaud	Subir Bairagi
Gene F. Kwan	Moïse Celicourt	Tarah Télusma Thelusme
George Psacharopoulos	Nicolas Allien	Tim Josling
Hans-Peter Kohler	Pantelis Koutroumpis	Travis J. Lybbert
Jacques Philippe Estime	Pierre Michel Chéry	Yvrose Guerrier
Jay Mackinnon	Rachel Nugent	

ADVISORY COUNCIL:

Camille Chalmers, State University of Haiti
Eddy Labossiere, President of Association of Haitian Economists
Kathleen Dorsainvil, formerly American University in D.C.
Pierre-Marie Boisson, Chairman of the Board of Directors of the SOGESOL

PANEL OF EMINENT ECONOMISTS

Kesner Pharel, prominent economist, public commentator and chairman and CEO of Group Croissance

Ketleen Florestal, advisor to the Executive Directors for Haiti at the Boards of the World Bank Group and the International Monetary Fund

Philomé Joseph Raymond Magloire, former Governor of the Central Bank of Haiti, specialist in finance and industrial economics

Vernon L Smith, professor of economics at Chapman University's Argyros School of Business and Economics and School of Law, and recipient of the Nobel Memorial Prize in Economic Sciences

How to Read this Book to Get the Most Out of It

This book is the result of our collaboration with more than 700 economists, experts, and researchers from Haiti and around the world, spanning sectors like education, governance, health, nutrition, infrastructure and so many more, to identify and shift attention to the best policies for Haiti, giving its citizens a better chance at a more prosperous future. Since resources are limited everywhere, we believe economic prioritization should be included in any serious debate about policy planning and decision-making for every country, not just Haiti.

Each of these short chapters was written in the first instance as a newspaper article and published in one of Haiti's leading newspapers, *Le Nouvelliste* or *Le National*. They have now been edited and refined for this book.

There are many ways you could read this book, the most obvious being from cover to cover. But if you're like most people, you probably have only a handful of policy areas that really matter to you. If that's the case, flip to the table of contents, find the policy areas that interest you, and go straight to the relevant chapters.

You don't have to read the chapters in any specific order to get the most out of the book, but we do think each chapter is worth the read. Our argument is simple: from a policy standpoint, challenge areas are usually complex. As a result, solutions in one area usually rely on and affect other areas.

For more information on the Haiti Priorise project, including the content of this book, please visit haitipriorise.com.

We hope that you enjoy reading this book as much as we enjoyed putting it together.

Thanks for reading!

Introduction

If you were in the fortunate position of being able to direct how a large sum of money was spent to improve Haiti's wellbeing and prosperity, what would you do?

Maybe you would focus on improving education? Research shows that this improves a nation's health and economy for generations. Or maybe your top concern would be healthcare, or water and sanitation? There are obviously many other issues like infrastructure, or disaster preparedness. Moreover, what should you do within these broad areas? Within education, should you first focus on higher education or pre-school? Should your first health focus be immunization or diabetes? Should disaster preparedness include some sort of armed forces to replace the United Nations Stabilization Mission in Haiti (MINUSTAH)?

When anybody tries to answer this question, all of us encounter the same problem: there is little information on the cost of such interventions and even less on the benefits.

We must base our answers on our own experience and emotions, or on our knowledge of one sector or another. These instincts are powerful and important. But they cannot replace data as a firm and fair foundation for important decision-making. Even strategic plans from the government or donors encounter this problem: there is a lack of comprehensive information about Haiti's challenges and the best solutions.

This book presents research from the landmark project, **Haiti Priorise**, that aims to fill some gaps in the data and provide new inputs for Haiti's discussion on priorities. Our goal in publishing this book is to create a valuable new resource not just for politicians and civic leaders, but for anyone with an interest in Haiti's future.

This project started with a series of 17 roundtable meetings across Haiti where we convened more than 500 sector experts, from government, business, civil society, academia and development organizations. Informed by the *Plan stratégique de développement d'Haïti*, these discussions reviewed Haiti's biggest challenges, and identified more than 1,000 investments that could help the nation.

Next, Haitian and international expert economists in dozens of areas were identified. They were asked to conduct research into the most promising solutions in their areas of expertise.

One big challenge for such a project is how to make investments comparable. *Haiti Priorise* has responded to this problem by using the well-established approach of cost-benefit analysis that is championed by the international think-tank, the Copenhagen Consensus Center, which has applied it to global and national challenges.

This approach reduces a complex policy or intervention to a clear, sharp set of figures: if we invest one extra gourde (or dollar, euro, or peso), we will get a return that is *x times* higher.

In this book, you will have the opportunity to review the researchers' evidence. Each chapter sets out the available data on the problem, and then shares the research findings.

Haiti Priorise researchers have not just tackled health problems, but have studied the environment, education, and the economy. They have asked questions like: what would be required to reach at least half of the population with 24-hour electricity? What are the benefits of setting up a legal aid system, or of digitizing national land records, or of teaching students in Creole? What could be achieved if we increased early childhood education, or improved rice production or roads?

The project, funded by the Canadian government, also saw all of the researchers present their findings to an eminent panel in Port-au-Prince.

This panel comprises very prominent Haitian economists Ketleen Florestal, Philomé Joseph Raymond Magloire, Kesner Pharel, and Nobel Prize-winning economist Vernon Smith. They studied the research, and suggested effective priorities for Haiti. At the same time, we gathered young Haitians to conduct the same exercise. In the final chapter of this book, you can find their recommendations.

We ask you, the reader, to consider your own views on the best options for Haiti, as you read this book. You may find compelling new economic arguments for policies that you already believe should be a priority. Or you may find your assumptions challenged by the evidence. We leave with you the data to provide answers to the vital question of how best to improve the nation's wellbeing and prosperity.

Bjorn Lomborg and Gaelle Prophete

Port au Prince

SOCIAL, ECONOMIC AND ENVIRONMENTAL
BENEFITS FOR EVERY GOURDE SPENT

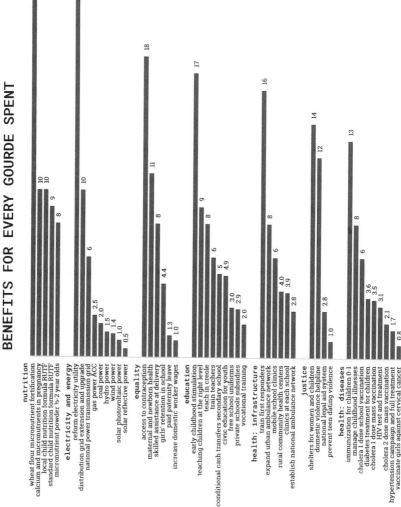

nutrition
- wheat flour micronutrient fortification — 24
- calcium and micronutrients in pregnancy — 10
- local child nutrition formula RUTF — 10
- standard child nutrition formula RUTF — 9
- micronutrient powder ½-2 year olds — 8

electricity and energy
- reform electricity utility — 22
- distribution grid extension and upgrade — 10
- national power transmission grid — 6
- gas power ACC — 2.5
- coal power — 2.0
- hydro power — 1.5
- wind power — 1.4
- solar photovoltaic power — 1.0
- solar reflective power — 0.5

equality
- access to contraception — 18
- maternal and newborn health — 11
- skilled assistance at delivery — 8
- girls' retention in school — 4.4
- paid paternity leave — 1.3
- increase domestic worker wages — 1.0

education
- early childhood stimulation — 17
- teaching children at the right level — 9
- teach in creole — 8
- train teachers — 6
- conditional cash transfers secondary school — 5
- civic education for youth — 4.9
- free school uniforms — 3.0
- private schools subsidies — 2.9
- vocational training — 2.0

health: infrastructure
- train first responders — 16
- expand urban ambulance network — 8
- mobile school clinics — 6
- rural community health centers — 4.0
- clinics at each school — 3.9
- establish national ambulance network — 2.8

justice
- shelters for women and children — 14
- domestic violence helpline — 12
- national legal aid system — 2.8
- prevent teen dating violence — 1.0

health: diseases
- immunization for children 0-1 — 13
- manage childhood illnesses — 8
- cholera 1 dose school vaccination — 6
- diabetes treatment for children — 3.6
- cholera 1 dose mass vaccination — 3.5
- HIV test and treatment — 3.1
- cholera 2 dose mass vaccination — 2.1
- hypertension campaign and full treatment — 1.7
- vaccinate girls against cervical cancer — 0.8

SOCIAL, ECONOMIC AND ENVIRONMENTAL
BENEFITS FOR EVERY GOURDE SPENT

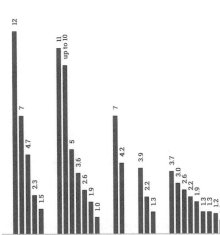

infrastructure
- expand mobile broadband — 12
- electronic port custom system — 7
- digitize government processes — 4.7
- road Gonaives to P-d-P — 2.3
- bridge Les Anglais — 1.5

government
- electronic registration of birth certificate — 11
- decentralized government — up to 10
- e-voting — 5
- performance pay in public service — 3.6
- digitize land records — 2.6
- national patrol force — 1.9
- increase public service pay 10% — 1.0

natural disasters
- flood early warning system — 7
- flood early warning system and shelters — 4.2

air pollution
- promote improved cookstoves — 3.9
- switch charcoal cookstoves to gas — 2.2
- switch wood cookstoves to gas — 1.3

agriculture
- subsidize fertilizer for rice — 3.7
- better agroforestry — 3.0
- crop transport truck system — 2.6
- biogas scale-up — 2.2
- introduce crop insurance — 1.9
- carbon pricing infrastructure — 1.3
- agricultural R&D — 1.3
- packaging and conservation center — 1.2
- 20% rice tariff for ten years — 0.8
- improved and intensified rice production — 0.8

poverty
- expand graduation program — 3.1
- off-grid hydro for village — 1.4
- off-grid diesel for village — 1.4
- diesel, solar and battery for village — 1.2
- expand microcredit program — 1.1

economy
- local content procurement — 2.2

water and sanitation
- rural borehole and handpump — 2.2
- rural community led total sanitation — 1.1
- urban container based sanitation — 1.0
- pit latrines in urban areas — 0.9

Haïti
priorise

Un plan de développement alternatif

All benefit-cost ratios are comparable. If you spend on promoting improved cookstoves, the social, economic and environmental benefits are 3.9 times the cost. Each gourde or dollar spent on expanding mobile broadband will do 12 gourdes or dollars of social and economic good.

In principle, all benefits are included. The benefits of providing electronic registration of birth certificate is not only time and cost savings, but also increased access to voting, finance and education.

Summaries and academic papers behind these numbers are available on www.haitipriorise.com

RESEARCH

COULD TARIFFS AND SUBSIDIES
BOOST THE ECONOMY?

Agriculture matters, both to Haiti and its new president. One of the biggest issues is tariffs and subsidies. Twenty years after tariffs were dropped, the impact continues to be discussed and debated.

An investment that is likely to be much-discussed is a ten-year, 20 percent import tariff on imports of American rice, which has been studied by Professor Tim Josling of Stanford University.

In the first year, a tariff would make farmers 1.7-2 billion gourdes (US$25-31.7 million) better off. It would provide 11.7 billion (US$170 million) of extra income over ten years. The government would collect 7.8 billion (US$114 million) in revenue in year one, and 57.8 billion gourdes (US$835 million) over a decade.

This sounds very positive. But surprisingly, the tariff would not do a lot to change the balance between domestic production and imports. Imports would still increase, and in ten years the expected harvest of Haitian rice would be 93,400 tons, compared to 84,900 tons without tariffs.

One reason for this is that there are many other challenges to increasing Haitian rice production, which the tariff wouldn't solve.

Moreover, what is good for farmers is not always good for consumers. Importers of 'Miami rice' would pass on the cost increase to the consumers. In total, Haitian shoppers would have to pay 7.9-9.9 billion (US$124-143 million) more for rice in the first year, and 72-79 billion gourdes (US$1.04-1.24 billion) over ten years. This impact could be reduced if the government used its new revenue to subsidize rice purchases making it cheaper for consumers. This would cut the overall cost increase to consumers to around 13.9 billion (US$202 million) but also entirely eliminate the revenue generated for the state.

Unfortunately, both with and without the state recycling the tariff back to the consumers, the policy would cost more to the Haitian economy than it would achieve. While it would benefit farmers, it would cost

11

the consumers even more, meaning every gourde spent would achieve less than one gourde in benefits.

However, a rice tariff could possibly become moderately cost-effective. If it were to encourage farmers to improve their farming practices and become more productive, benefits would increase. However, the rice yield would need to increase by 20% for the benefits to begin to exceed the costs.

Professor Josling also studies how crop insurance could help Haitian farmers. Creating a simple insurance scheme could allow farmers to aim for higher yields because they would have a safety net when harvests are poor, with a guaranteed minimum income. The research finds that this policy could achieve a modest amount of good.

Experience shows that compensating farmers from bad luck with insurance encourages extra risk-taking, which increases rice yields. Somewhere between 9 and 17 percent more rice would be produced in good years, according to the scenarios envisaged by Professor Josling.

The costs include startup costs, recurring costs, payments to farmers in poor years, and the premiums paid by farmers themselves (around 1,400 or $20 per hectare).

Total start-up costs for the scheme are 13.8 million (US$200,000), with additional costs of 6.9 million gourdes (US$100,000) and 3.4 million gourdes (US$50,000) in the next two years, respectively, and a recurring cost of 3.4 million gourdes (US$50,000). Insurance premiums would cost 9.4 million (US$137,000) in year one, rising slowly after that. Payouts would be in the region of 1.2 billion gourdes (US$17.5 million), when compensation is due. In total, the costs would run to 6.2 billion gourdes (US$90 million) over a decade. But it would increase yields, meaning an average higher annual income of more than 692 million (US$13 million). In total, including the insurance payouts, the benefits over a decade would run to 12.1 billion gourdes (US$175 million). Professor Josling finds that each gourde spent will produce almost two gourdes of good.

A third policy emerges from his scrutiny with even higher marks: paying fertilizer subsidies to rice farmers. The subsidy would be worth half the market price for five years, and then decline by 10% increments to zero in year 10.

The proposed subsidy would cost 1.8 billion gourdes (US$27.4 million) in the first year, and the extra fertilizer would cost 608 million gourdes (US$8.8 million).

It is estimated that fertilizer sales would rise from 750 to 1,132 tons in the first year, while the cost to farmers would fall from 2.4 billion gourdes (US$36 million) to 1.2 billion gourdes (US$18.6 million). Farm income would increase by 53 percent, as the rice harvest increases from 147,000 tons to 225,000 tons. The extra rice produced would be worth 7.8 billion gourdes (US$112.6 million), and the reduction of the cost of fertilizer would be worth 1.2 billion gourdes (US$18.6 million). Over a decade, the costs will run to about 16.3 billion gourdes (US$236 million), with about two-thirds for subsidies and one-third for buying extra fertilizer. The benefit will amount to 61 billion gourdes (US$884 million) over the decade, with about 10% from lower fertilizer costs and 90% from increased rice production. In total, each gourde will achieve 3.7 gourdes of good subsidizing fertilizer.

However, a word of caution on how to organize the fertilizer subsidy to actually get the benefits. Haiti has not had positive experiences with fertilizer subsidies since 2000, points out independent consultant Joel Le Turioner in an expert commentary. Even subsidies of up to 50% did not help the development of fertilizer use in Haiti. Audits showed cronyism in distribution of subsidized fertilizer leading to its misappropriation. And because the subsidized fertilizer was bought and distributed by the state, often at short notice, other sellers imported less than they could have used out of fear of being stuck with unsubsidized, unsellable fertilizer.

This tells us that any policy needs to be carefully designed. Subsidies must be distributed in a way that prevents future cronyism and misappropriation, while allowing farmers access to more fertilizer. This could be achieved with subsidies taking the form of vouchers, giving control to farmers. This setup has been demonstrated in several projects with the Ministry of Agriculture, Natural Resources and Rural Development (MARNDR). Using such vouchers, Haiti can ensure that subsidized fertilizer won't underperform like it has previously, but could help grow agriculture to produce more, and generate future benefits worth nearly 4 gourdes for each gourde spent.

This would help to expand the agricultural economy, and be good for all of Haiti.

Intervention	Benefit	Cost	BCR
Rice tariff	11.8 billion gourdes (US$170.5 million)	14 billion gourdes (US$202.5 million)	0.8
Crop insurance	12.1 billion gourdes (US$175 million)	9.5 billion gourdes (US$137.7 million)	1.9
Fertilizer subsidy	61 billion gourdes (US$883.9 million)	16.3 billion gourdes (US$235.9 million)	3.7
SRI-A to improve rice productivity in Artibonite	2.9 billion gourdes (US$43 million)	3.9 billion gourdes (US$57 million)	0.8
Investment in Ag. R&D with 50% adoption	33 billion gourdes (US$487 million)	29 billion gourdes (US$418 million)	1.1
Optimal agro-silviculture	926 billion gourdes (US$13 billion)	321 billion gourdes (US$4.6 billion)	3

All figures use a discount rate of 5%.

14

TOUGH CHOICES TO IMPROVE HAITI'S EMERGENCY RESPONSE NETWORK

Hundreds or even thousands of lives could be saved every year by improving the ambulance network, or by training paramedics and first aid volunteers.

In Haiti in 2013 and 2014, more than half-a-million accidents and emergencies resulted in 9000 deaths. Fewer than two percent were attended by free ambulances.

Improving the emergency response system is a challenge for many developing nations. Trauma patients are six-times more likely to die in low-income countries than in rich ones.

The Haitian ambulance system comprises the free *Centre Ambulancier National* (CAN) and two private providers. Free ambulance use is limited by the CAN base's centralized location in Port-au- Prince, a small number of personnel, limited equipment, mountainous terrain, and fewer than one hundred ambulances.

Applied Economist at the Ministry of Public Health and Population, Contracting Unit R. Christina Daurisca finds that one approach to this challenge could be to first build an urban ambulance system. This would serve around half of Haiti's population.

Using Public Investment Project data and 2016-2017 budgets of the National Ambulance Centre, Daurisca examines the costs of setting up 18 urban ambulance centers with 176 ambulances. This would provide 33 ambulances for every million urban inhabitants.

Each ambulance would be served by 9 workers, plus supervisors and a central operations center, for a total cost of 561 million gourdes. Around 2500 lives would be saved every year.

Using cost-benefit analysis – a research method that allows the comparison of social, environmental, and health benefits of contrasting policy options – Daurisca concludes that the reduction in death and injury and improvements to productivity and the economy would be worth nearly 8-times more than the cost.

Creating a nationwide ambulance system that covers the entire country would obviously be the gold-standard policy. But reaching the most remote parts of Haiti would be very expensive.

Adding to the urban network with another 99 ambulances per every million rural inhabitants requires another 569 ambulances. A nationwide ambulance system would save nearly 4,000 lives each year – but for a very high price of 2.3 billion gourdes. Each gourde would now only achieve less than three gourdes worth of good.

Our natural reaction is to choose the policy option that saves the most lives. But we must contrast this with other ways to use limited funds – whether it's expanding childhood immunization, or improving girls' education, or implementing an electronic voting system. At the end of the day, not every policy can be pursued at once. What do you think should be the top priority? *Haiti Priorise* aims to help shape conversation by highlighting the solutions that can do the most good.

To the challenge of a poor ambulance network, Daurisca identifies an alternative way to reduce the death toll nationwide: educating more paramedics and first responders.

Firstly, this approach means providing several days of first aid training to 27,000 community members such as traditional midwives and teachers. Secondly, 550 professional paramedics would be given ten days of training. The cost would be just 80 million gourdes in the first year, and this would save around 700 lives every year. Each gourde spent will produce 16 gourdes of social good.

Daurisca notes that a combination of an urban network and community training may have the highest absolute rewards, but of course would also be significantly expensive.

Any improvements to the ambulance network must be integrated with improvements to healthcare access. Ambulances take patients to hospitals, where cost can sometimes be a factor.

In a country with seismic risk and weather events, expansion of paramedic and first responder training deserves sustained support.

Intervention	Benefit	Cost	BCR
Urban Ambulance network	4,406,893,345	561,559,893	7.8
National ambulance network	6,587,200,390	2,320,046,967	2.8
First responders and paramedics	1,266,324,056	80,369,344	15.8

CUTTING HAITI'S
UNDER-FIVE CHILD DEATH RATE

Haiti has the highest rate of child mortality in the Americas – far higher even than other poor countries. For every 1,000 children born, 52 will not survive to their first birthday, and 69 will not reach 5 years of age. The greatest tragedy about this is that many of these deaths are entirely preventable.

Haiti saw a sharp increase in the under-five mortality rate following the catastrophic 2010 earthquake. There will be an estimated 7,760 child deaths in 2017 – or 49 deaths per day.

Lower respiratory infections and diarrheal diseases together claim more than 8,500 lives of kids aged under five each year – a toll that we should be able to almost entirely eliminate, through increased immunization and basic care. Respiratory infections are responsible for one-third of all deaths of children between the age of 1 month and the age of five, while diarrheal diseases account for another 16 percent.

In new research for the project *Haiti Priorise*, for which specialist economists look at different ways to respond to diverse developmental, environmental, health, and economic challenges in the country, Dr. Karin Stenberg of the World Health Organization and colleagues Ludovic Queuille of the Pan-American Health Organization, Rachel Sanders of Avenir Health, Marcus Cadet of the Ministry of Public Health and Population, study ways to reduce the death-toll of children between the ages of one month and five years. (The main causes of death among newborns are dealt with by interventions delivered around birth, and the researchers have written a separate analysis to examine the interventions that reach pregnant mothers and babies in their first month of life.)

The solutions are simple and well understood: Immunization can prevent the conditions that result in illness and death among children. Immunization needs to be expanded, to save more lives. And common causes of the illnesses that result in death – such as diarrhea and pneumonia – can be both managed and treated.

The authors' analysis delves into the costs and the health benefits of increasing coverage of immunization from its current levels (which vary depending on which illness is being targeted) to 80% or 95% in 2018, and maintaining this level until 2036.

The interventions are delivered through population-and community based approaches as well as primary level care. The researchers make the point that some other healthcare investments in Haiti could be quite limited by health system capacity constraints, but under-five interventions can more easily overcome these problems, because they are less reliant on having staff with highly specialized skills.

The authors argue that in Haiti, allowing community-based care to play a large role in the provision of integrated management of childhood illness needs to be a key strategy, as current health workforce numbers are far below recommended minimum benchmarks. Their model still assumes a significant share of service delivery would happen at primary level facilities though, so accessibility to health facilities does need to improve to expand coverage.

The projected additional investment over the years 2018-2036 varies between US$8 and $100 million depending on the scope of the package and the target coverage. The average annual per capita cost ranges from just USD 0.72 cents for expanding routine immunization to US$8.26 for the expanded immunization combined with proper management of childhood illnesses.

The implementation of a comprehensive package of both preventive and curative care could save over 71,000 child lives between 2018 and 2036, if it were made universally available (meaning 95% coverage), and this would bring the under-five mortality ratio down from its current level of 69 per 1000 live births by 62 percent, to reach 51 deaths per 1000 live births, which would make Haiti's death-toll closer to the average for developing nations.

The researchers make the case that immunization provides an example of a health service for which, even in the short term, money can overcome poor system capacity. While adding new vaccines to the immunization schedule is costly, such a package creates benefits for society that are higher than the costs.

The greatest absolute gains in terms of deaths averted and reduction in mortality rates come from management of common childhood illness. This is partially due to the lower starting coverage of these interventions.

Other poor nations in the Americas, including Bolivia and Honduras, have succeeded in lowering their under-five death rates, and Haiti can too. We know what is needed to save these lives; what is needed now is a concerted focus on doing so.

Package	Target Coverage	Benefit	Cost	BCR
Package 1. Routine Expanded Programme on Immunization 2015	80%	US$25.9 billion	US$2.8 billion	9.4
	95%	US$47.3 billion	US$4.5 billion	10.4
Package 2. Routine Expanded Programme on Immunization 2015 + Pneumococcal conjugate vaccine (scenario A)*	80%	US$51.7 billion	US$16 billion	3.2
	95%	US$74.2 billion	US$20 billion	3.7
Package 2. Routine Expanded Programme on Immunization 2015 + Pneumococcal conjugate vaccine (scenario B)**	80%	US$51.7 billion	US$12 billion	4.3
	95%	US$74.2 billion	US$15 billion	4.9
Package 3. Management of common childhood illness	80%	US$95.3 billion	US$15 billion	6.3
	95%	US$129 billion	US$19 billion	6.8
Package 4. Combination Expanded Programme on Immunization 2015 + Pneumococcal conjugate vaccine + management of common childhood illness	80%	US$130 billion	US$31 billion	4.3
	95%	US$172 billion	US$38 billion	4.5

* *Price for PCV-13 estimated at USD 17 per dose.*
** *Price for PCV-13 estimated at USD 3.3 per dose.*
All figures use a discount rate of 5%.

SKILLS TRAINING AND
CIVICS EDUCATION
TO MAKE 'BETTER' CITIZENS

Nations have a short opportunity during which they can impart skills to any child, to prepare him or her for adulthood. What is better: to teach a trade in the hope of providing greater economic security, or to teach civic education with the goal of making a 'better' citizen? Vocational training certainly sounds like it should be a high priority. If students learn a particular trade, they can make money from this trade after graduation. Every economy needs plumbers, carpenters or electricians. This logic dominated the approach to education in the 1960s and 1970s in most countries.

However, Professor George Psacharopolous of Georgetown University finds that many studies have demonstrated that this did not really work. Sometimes, the problem was that graduates did not find relevant employment. Vocational training is more expensive than general education, but both often have a similar impact on future earnings. Many countries and donors have moved away from vocational training.

In Haiti, vocational training would be relatively expensive. Overseas evidence suggests it would be about 50 percent more expensive than general education. Professor Psacharopolous estimates that providing three years of vocational training after secondary school would cost around 440,000 gourdes ($6,370) per student per year. Training 1,000 students would cost 440 million gourdes ($6.37 million). There is also a cost to the students themselves, who could have earned money in the workforce instead of training.

But once they graduate, vocational education graduates can earn around 50% more than their counterparts who dropped out after primary school. The Institut Haitien de Statistique et Informatique (IHSI) at the Ministere de l'Economie et des Finances conducted an Enquête sur les Conditions de Vie des Ménages après Séisme, which found that the annual mean income of an adult with primary school education is around 110,000 gourdes (about $1500), and someone with lower secondary school training is around 127,000 gourdes ($1800). Professor Psacharopoulos finds that vocational training would lead to an average income of about 161,000 gourdes ($2300). This lift in income occurs across his or her entire working life.

When we compare the rather costly extra vocational training and the lost wages during training with the higher productivity of the graduates for the rest of their lives, we find that every gourde spent on vocational training will generate returns to Haiti worth around two gourdes. This is quite a respectable return.

Introducing civics education classes, similarly, sounds like a worthwhile investment. It has been established that improving civic behavior leads to a more coherent society, more stability, less conflict, and better participation in voting. A lot of evidence shows that more education means lower crime rates.

Professor Psacharopoulos assumes that adding a two-year civics course to the curriculum would increase the cost of secondary education by about half of the cost of general education each year. For each student, this would mean an annual expense of around 19,500 gourdes ($280).

There is little information on the efficiency of civics education generally, and none from Haiti. However, studies in the UK indicate that civics education enhances earnings by between 1% and 6%. Thus, Professor Psacharopoulos suggests there could be a 3% earnings boost in Haiti. Taking this into account, every gourde spent on civics education would achieve about 5 gourdes worth of good.

A third option would be to create one year of compulsory vocational and civics training for 15-year olds who drop out of secondary school but don't go on to upper secondary school. Professor Psacharopoulos estimates every gourde spent would achieve about three gourdes worth of benefits to Haiti.

Studies have found that increased societal trust – which civics education could contribute to – improves economic growth. So there could be additional benefits to these investments that are difficult to estimate but nonetheless should be considered when making priorities for education.

But even with this caveat, Professor Psacharopoulos points out that other education interventions might bring higher returns to society relative to vocational and civics training. Based on rigorous international research, these might include improving the education of girls, improving basic education, and especially increasing early childhood education access.

Intervention	Benefit	Cost	BCR
Vocational training	899,000 gourdes (US$13,000)	440,000 gourdes (US$6,370)	2
Civics	96,000 gourdes (US$1,380)	19,500 gourdes (US$280)	4.9
Gap year of vocational and civics	179,000 gourdes (US$2,600)	69,000 gourdes (US$1,000)	2.6

All figures use a discount rate of 5%.

DECENTRALIZATION AND REDUCING POST-HARVEST LOSSES: IDEAS WHOSE TIME HAS COME?

There are as many different ideas to improve the wellbeing of Haiti as there are Haitians. After talking to more than 700 people to identify all the nation's biggest challenges and most promising solutions, we asked specialist economist researchers to focus on 85 key ideas across topics from health to infrastructure to the environment.

Here are two ideas that have been long-discussed in Haiti. Are they ideas whose time has come?

The first research, by Tarah Télusma Thelusme, Statistics Department Manager at the Public Investment Unit at the Ministry of Planning and External Cooperation, focuses on the implementation of existing laws on decentralization.

There are many different types of decentralization. In political decentralization, subnational units are endowed with the power to make decisions about local governance issues, with political representatives at a national level. In administrative decentralization, government operations remain centralized and delegates are posted at subnational level. And in fiscal decentralization, subnational units have autonomy where it concerns the power to tax and collect revenues.

The Haitian constitution has provisions for all three of these types of decentralization, but not all have been put into practice.

On paper, municipalities have a lot of power to tax and collect user fees, borrow, and accept mandatory transfers from the central authority.

These transfers come from a fund managed by the Ministry of the Interior, called the 'Local Government Management and Development Fund' (*Fonds de gestion et de développement des collectivités territoriales*). It is replenished from a number of central government operations and is believed to be significant. However, it is not known how much goes to subnational units, nor how it is spent.

The legal framework specifies that technical councils are meant to help the municipality administratively and technically. Thelusme suggests that the establishment of the technical councils could improve the capacity of municipalities, and the quality of services to citizens such as water and sanitation services, vocational and technical education, maintenance of public spaces and management services. Municipalities should also be able to collect revenue from property taxes and cattle activity.

Placing technical councils at municipal level would cost 5.6 billion gourdes; training would cost 18.7 million, and allocations to units would cost another 6.4 billion gourdes. The total costs are 10-12 billion gourdes.

However, decentralization also means that local authorities can better fit services to local needs. Therefore, research shows that more decentralization generally is associated with citizen satisfaction. Translating this satisfaction into monetary terms is difficult, but Thelusme's research suggests benefits worth in the region of 106 billion gourdes. This means every gourde invested in enforcing existing law on decentralization would have benefits worth 10 gourdes.

A second research paper focuses on how to reduce the losses experienced between farm and market. This has been a real concern for the agricultural industry for some time. Losses are estimated at more than 50%-60% of production. This is, amongst other things, the result of inadequate infrastructure to facilitate market access for high-quality agricultural products.

Poor transport options and a lack of adequate storage infrastructure mean that fruit and vegetables spoil on the spot, and farmers are pressured into selling their products immediately after harvest. This leads to large price fluctuations during the year and the sale of low quality products.

Middle-men (*madan sara*) buy produce from producers and carry them to urban markets. Unfortunately, the transportation used by the madan sara presents high risks.

Romy Reggiani Theodat of the Ministry of Commerce and Industry (MCI) looks at two complementary proposals: introducing a crop transport truck system, and creating a packaging and conservation center.

Both proposals would prioritize the fruit and vegetable sector, and focus on three important regions: the Saint-Raphael commune and the Sud and Artibonite departments.

Theodat suggests that one way to improve transportation of perishable and delicate products to markets is by making specialized trucks available to driver associations.

This would be very expensive: on an annual basis, the cost would be 6.31 billion gourdes (US$92 million). The benefits, though, from the reduction in post-harvest losses and boost to the agricultural sector, would be worth 2.6 gourdes for every gourde spent, or 16.17 billion gourdes (US$237 million) annually.

A sorting, conditioning and preservation facility, along with a quality control system for producer associations in harvesting areas, would be more expensive. Setting up and maintaining three centers would cost 7.48 billion gourdes (US$109 million) spread if the cost were spread out evenly over each year. The benefits would be worth slightly more than one gourde for every gourde that is spent.

Intervention	Benefit	Cost	BCR
Decentralized Government	106 billion gourdes (US$1.65 billion)	12 billion gourdes (US$190 million)	10.2
Crop Transport Truck System	8.9 billion gourdes (US$140 million)	6.3 billion gourdes (US$100 million)	2.6
Packaging and Conservation Center	16.2 billion gourdes (US$250 million)	7.5 billion gourdes (US$120 million)	1.2

All figures use a discount rate of 5%.

ELECTRONIC VOTING:
A SOLUTION FOR THE FUTURE?

In Haiti, the rate of participation in elections is low. Less than a quarter of eligible voters participated in last October's elections. The manipulations of the ballots are numerous and their treatment tedious, which creates so many opportunities for errors and frauds. Voting, counting, stripping and tabulating the vote is exhausting and binding, by the traditional method.

Meanwhile, the costs of holding an election have climbed more than 400% in 25 years, from less than 880 million gourdes (US$13 million) in 1990 to 4.4 billion gourdes (US$66 million) in 2015.

With apparently broad levels of public support, electronic voting is one way of reducing this cost, cutting the opportunities for errors and fraud, and re-establishing public trust.

Electronic Voting, as the name implies, is recorded and processed via an electronic system. In some forms, electronic voting could even possibly be used to allow engagement from members of the Diaspora.

Based on the global trend towards the dematerialization of transactions and the success in Haiti in record time of the cell phone, it is possible to believe that electronic voting is the future.

But how realistic is that vision of the future – and what could it look like in reality? Executive director of Xtra Consult, Pierre Michel Chéry analyzed the feasibility of electronic voting in Haiti.

One of the chief reasons that electronic voting is on the agenda in Haiti is that it is seen to be likely to boost confidence in election results – and thereby participation.

But electronic voting would also save money: there would be no need to print and transport millions of electoral ballots. Processing times would also be much shorter.

One option is the use of mobile phone technology. While this seems attractive because of the reach of mobile phones, it is likely that it would create new concerns about the results, because it would be relatively difficult to verify the identity of voters.

The option that Chéry explores is using Electronic Voting Machines would be more traditional because voters still have go to a voting office. The electronic voting machines would be linked to a regional or national server. The innovation is that machines could be configured with a double verification system using voter ID numbers and fingerprints, limiting fraudulent votes and other irregularities. The voter would receive a receipt, either for their own records or to drop into a voting urn.

Chéry's research shows that a dual-check electronic voting system for Haiti would cost around 1.1 billion Haitian gourdes (US$17 million).

This money would purchase 10,950 voting machines, along with computers, hardware and software, and ensure there were enough trained personnel to operate the system. The equipment and materials amortize over 5 years, essentially meaning new machines would be needed every presidential election cycle. This is something to bear in mind: electronic voting requires ongoing investment.

However, the money spent would make Haitian elections more efficient. E-voting would save about 1.7 billion gourdes (US$26 million) in expenditure. It would eliminate spending on ballot printing (worth 880 million gourdes or US$13 million), as well as management of the tabulation center (271 million gourdes or US$4 million). This could mean a reduction in dependence on foreign aid.

Moreover, the research shows that electronic voting would create gains worth US$6 million just by shortening the time between the different stages of the electoral process.

In total, the research concludes that the benefits of implementing an electronic voting system would be 5.3 times higher than the costs. So, every gourde spent would generate 5.30 gourdes of social good.

However, this is no silver bullet that would generate a watertight voting system overnight. Experience suggests that switching to electronic voting can take about ten years, from the time of pilot tests to a complete overhaul of the system.

We also need to recall that manual voting today provides some 50,000 short-term jobs. By switching to electronic voting, many of those jobs would be lost, but others would be created, involving higher qualified staff.

The advantages of electronic voting are clear: it is more efficient and costs less than today's manual system. It is more transparent and reliable and could pave the way for digitizing public administration and governance across Haiti.

Two big questions that remain are: should it be a top priority for Haiti over other investments that could strengthen democracy and institutions? And would electronic voting be enough to re-establish Haitian voter confidence?

Based on the global trend towards the dematerialization of transactions and the success in Haiti in record time of the cell phone, it is possible to believe that electronic voting is the future.

Intervention	Benefit	Cost	BCR
E-voting	$91 million	$17 million	5.3

All figures use a discount rate of 5%.

PLAYING DIGITAL CATCH-UP:
FINDING OPPORTUNITIES FOR HAITI

The digital revolution affects many aspects of our lives – evident from this article's availability online to readers anywhere in the world, or the ubiquity of cellphones that many of us cannot live without.

But Internet coverage in Haiti remains limited and expensive. Just four percent of households have access, and fewer than 1% of Haitians have mobile Internet. Some government processes that are digitized elsewhere are still done here in the old-fashioned way. This reduces opportunities for Haitians and slows down economic growth. Haiti could be richer with faster Internet and more digitization.

Dr. Pantelis Koutroumpis, Research Fellow at Imperial College Business School, says what Haiti really needs is a holistic National Broadband Plan with targets for coverage, capacity, and competition. In its absence, he proposes improving the infrastructure that powers Haiti's Internet, along with the government's processes.

Dr. Koutroumpis's first proposal is to install a second under-sea cable to generate faster Internet speeds. This will boost mobile broadband access from less than 1% today, to 50 percent by 2021.

Each kilometer of cable costs $90,000 (5.7 million gourdes). It would need to cover around 250kms, so the cable's price is $22.5 million dollars (1.4 billion gourdes). The Internet transmission would cost an increasing amount each year, hitting $14 million (890 million gourdes) in 2021.

In all, this investment would require $56.1 billion (3.56 trillion gourdes) – so it is not cheap.

The increased connectivity combined with improved connection speeds (3G/4G) and low prices will help start new businesses that digitize everyday activities, while individuals will be able to better monitor their business activities and interact with the government.

Dr. Koutroumpis predicts the increase in Internet speed will boost Haitian economic growth each year by 0.1 percent. That may not sound like a lot, but in the year 2021 it means Haiti will be about $60 million (4 billion gourdes) richer.

More money will be made each year in earnings from internet connections. In total, every gourde spent on this initiative is expected to bring benefits worth 12 gourdes.

The second approach is to digitize bureaucratic processes. Dr. Koutroumpis zeroes in on a range of examples where he finds digitization could make a lot of difference.

Currently, it takes 97 days to register a new business and 6-9 months to register property, both a lot longer than the Latin America and Caribbean average. These inefficiencies cost money and time.

By digitizing the processes, Dr. Koutroumpis estimates that the time taken to start a business could be cut to 12 days, and property registration to just 11 days. Similarly, he suggests setting up a credit bureau to increase and improve access to finance from 1.6% to 20% of small- and medium-sized businesses.

There would be set-up costs associated with these digitization initiatives, but there would be benefits. For every gourde spent across digitization endeavors, the research estimates that there would be nearly 5 gourdes of benefit to Haiti.

A second researcher focuses on a specific area where digitization could help Haiti: the civil registration system.

Moïse Celicourt, Economics Professor at the University Notre Dame of Haiti (UNDH) finds that nearly 30% of children aged under four do not have a certificate of birth registration. This deprives the child of fundamental rights and it risks condemning him or her to exclusion in society.

Prof. Celicourt proposes computerization of the birth registration process to provide birth certificates to all newborns, and children up to the age of four.

The civil registry has already started undergoing a process of modernization, which culminated in the creation of the National Identification Office, whose mission is to identify all Haitians from birth. However, this is focused on registering adults.

Because most Haitian mothers give birth at home, registering a child can be a time-consuming process involving repeated travel to registry offices.

More than 340,000 young children have no birth certificates. Prof. Celicourt's proposal would affect 2 million children.

The intervention would cost $12 million (760 million gourdes), with an initial cost of $800,000 in the first year of implementation. Basically, this would improve the computer equipment at the civil registry offices.

Digitization would save the applicants time and transportation costs, and would save the government money. In financial terms, these benefits would each be worth around $3–4 million (190–250 million gourdes).

But the benefits would continue throughout the children's lives: they would be guaranteed the right to vote, and access to the financial system.

The benefits vary depending on whether a lack of birth certificates is preventing children from going to school. While education regulations stipulate that students cannot sit state exams without a birth certificate, it is difficult to gauge whether this is enforced. If it does happen, then each gourde spent on this initiative could create benefits worth ten gourdes to society. If it is not a widespread practice, the benefits are considerably lower – although it is safe to assume that there is potential in the system for corruption, which birth certificates would eliminate.

While today Haiti is behind other countries on Internet access, these investments would help it to catch up, and compete in the digital age.

Intervention	Benefit	Cost	BCR
Increase mobile broadband penetration to 50% in 5 years; install an undersea cable to support the increased traffic	686 billion gourdes (US$10.7 billion)	56 billion gourdes (US$870 million)	12
Significant digitization of government processes	559 billion gourdes (US$8.7 billion)	120 billion gourdes (US$1.9 billion)	4.7
Electronic birth certificate registration	18 billion gourdes (US$280 million)	1.7 billion gourdes (US$30 million)	Up to 10.5

All figures use a discount rate of 5%.

REDUCING DOMESTIC VIOLENCE
HELPS ALL OF HAITI

Domestic violence is a human rights issue, a public health issue, and an economic development issue.

In Haiti, evidence from confidential surveys suggests that domestic violence is a serious problem: it appears that around 273,200 women suffer from severe physical and/or sexual violence per year. This adds up to 9.4 per cent of the population of 14–49 year-old women.

Domestic violence has considerable consequences. It not only causes pain and suffering for the victims but creates costs for society. Victims are more likely to commit suicide, have more unwanted pregnancies, are less likely to complete education, are less likely to seek employment, are more likely to have underweight babies, and are more likely to contract sexually transmitted diseases including HIV.

This stops victims from fulfilling their potential and makes them less likely to be employed. Thus, it has far reaching consequences for societal development.

Dr. Anke Hoeffler from the University of Oxford studies the costs and effects of investments to reduce domestic violence.

One policy Dr. Hoeffler looks at is re-building the women's shelter in the West which was destroyed during the earthquake of 2010, and finds that this would be a very good investment.

Haiti has had shelters in four departments (North, Northeast, South-East and West) to accommodate victims of violence. Forensic, psychosocial, legal and social services are provided at these shelters, which are all managed by women's organizations, with the Ministry for Women's Affairs and Women's Rights (MCFDF) playing a coordinating role.

The MCFDF is currently trying to raise funds for the construction of a new shelter. Dr. Hoeffler estimates that the building costs and operating costs for 30 years would add up to 10.2 million gourdes. Her research suggests that each year the shelter will save one life, and the equivalent of 12 years lost due to injury and illness caused by domestic violence.

Using the cost-benefit approach of Haiti Priorise, Dr. Hoeffler puts this into economic terms, and finds that every gourde spent on the shelter would generate returns worth 14 gourdes.

She also looks at a longer-term approach: teaching teenagers about safe and healthy relationships. There is evidence from other countries that this decreases the incidence of sexual assault, increases knowledge of domestic violence, and reduces violence among teenagers.

The goal would be to reach 18,800 youths – about 8 percent of all 14-year olds. This means 157 teachers would need to be trained. Based on a pilot program, it is estimated that the costs would involve three days of training and five days of implementation. As well as delivery costs, there is the cost of the use of outside experts and production of the study materials.

It is expected that there would be an impact on teen domestic violence for four years. It is also assumed that after four years there will be some positive effects, such as reduced substance use, depression, and self-harm, which have been associated with teen dating violence prevention programs.

Unfortunately, the cost of paying teachers to teach this curriculum outside school hours in Haiti makes the delivery of this intervention very expensive. So, in cost-benefit terms, every gourde spent on this initiative would generate benefits worth just one gourde.

Another approach could be to introduce a national helpline for victims of domestic violence. These are popular in some countries and, in some cases, phone calls increase dramatically in response to public campaigns. However, there is little evidence as to how well they work.

The costs of a helpline would be renting an office, operations costs and staffing. An information campaign would also be needed, to target women aged 15-49 and make them aware of the helpline. This would add up to 14.65 million gourdes.

Although there is scant data, Dr. Hoeffler assumes that a helpline would avoid one per cent of deaths caused by domestic violence, as well as time lost to illness and injury caused by IPV. In economic terms, it is likely that every gourde spent would achieve benefits worth around 12 gourdes.

The effects of domestic violence are felt every day in Haiti, in lower economic productivity, unnecessary health costs, and misery. Tackling domestic violence should be a priority.

Intervention	Benefit	Cost	BCR
Shelter	143 million gourdes (US$2.2 million)	10.2 million gourdes (US$0.16 million)	14
Helpline	176 million gourdes (US$2.7 billion)	14.6 million gourdes (US$0.23 billion)	12
Prevention of Dating Violence	36 million gourdes (US$0.56 million)	35 million gourdes (US$0.54 million)	1

All figures use a discount rate of 5%.

EARLY CHILDHOOD EDUCATION: AN INVESTMENT IN HAITI'S FUTURE

Investment in education is essential for Haiti to lift incomes and fight poverty. But in this area like every other, decision-makers face many options. How can limited resources be spent to achieve the most possible? Well-known education economist Atonu Rabbani makes the point that one of the most powerful education investments that can be made is in early childhood education.

Professor Rabbani has analyzed early childhood education around the world. He finds that it creates lifelong effects for the children who receive it. It lifts incomes substantially, decreases the chance of incarceration, and reduces the impact of negative things like nutritional deficiencies.

He proposes a simple policy where Haitian children aged 4–5 years old at the pre-primary school level receive early childhood education for two years in small groups of 25. Each group requires two trained ECE facilitators along with a helper. Although called "education", the intervention includes teacher-led activities involving toys and the development of social skills through games.

Currently, Haiti has about 516,000 children aged 4 and 5 years. It seems feasible to reach about half of this population, or around 258,000 children per year.

This could cost as little as 5,500 gourdes (US$79) per student per year. This intervention increases the chances that children will spend more time in schooling later, so we need to consider that cost, too. This gives us a total cost per year of 6.9 billion gourdes (US$100 million).

Based on a famous, long-term research experiment in Jamaica, there is good evidence that such a policy will lead to an increase of 35 percent in earnings for the children, from the age they start working at around 16. For someone earning today's average of around 63,000 gourdes (US$910), it would mean an additional 22,000 gourdes (US$320) per year. For one cohort of children, that adds up to about 115 billion gourdes (US$1.6 billion) in today's money.

36

The return on investment is considerable: for every gourde that Haiti spends on early childhood education, the benefits are worth 17 gourdes.

Professor Rabbani makes the point that while it is important to start investing in education as early as possible, it is also important to continue the investment later.

Haiti has made progress promoting school attendance. Professor Rabbani suggests that an important additional area of focus could be lifting the quality of primary education.

In Kenya and India, putting students into groups according to their learning level has improved performance.

This requires students to be tracked according to their achievement levels (as measured through, say, test scores in language or mathematics), grouped, and put into special classes alongside their regular classes.

The program would target about 870,000 children in primary school.

The costs would add up to about 28 billion gourdes (US$390 million). Again, this is expected to lift incomes when children grow up, by about 12,000 gourdes (US$170) a year, leading to benefits worth 235 billion gourdes (US$3.3 billion). So, every gourde spent would generate benefits worth nine gourdes.

Finally, Professor Rabbani suggests using payments to parents to prevent their children dropping out of secondary school. These are known as 'conditional cash transfers.' Among the children who start sixth grade, only 30 percent eventually finish. Dr. Rabbani suggests paying around 8,300 gourdes (US$120) per child per year to the poorest households, for students between the ages of 11 and 15, if they stay in school. The program would cost around 31,000 (US$550) gourdes per child over five years, from both payments and extra schooling costs. For the complete program, the cost is 16 billion gourdes (US$230 million). On average, his research suggests this would lead to one extra year of schooling for each student, which means an income boost, along with the help to the poorest families. In total, the benefits are worth 5 gourdes for every gourde spent.

All the proposals have a great return on investment – but all also involve up-front costs, for large future impacts. What this means is that investments today could reap large benefits for many years to come.

Intervention	Benefit	Cost	BCR
Two-Year Early Childhood Interventions at the Pre-Primary Phase	115 billion gourdes (US$1.8 billion)	6.9 billion gourdes (US$110 million)	14
Teaching children at the right level	235 billion gourdes (US$3.7 billion)	27 billion gourdes (US$420 million)	9
CCT for Secondary Level Children	89 billion gourdes (US$1.4 billion)	16 billion gourdes (US$250 million)	5

All figures use a discount rate of 5%.

POWERING HAITI'S HOUSEHOLDS

Electricity reaches less than one-quarter of Haiti. This is an obstacle to economic and social development.

Today, the biggest obstacles to the development of the electricity sector in Haiti are the weakness of institutions, systems, and poverty. Many people take electricity without paying for it, severely affecting the income of the EDH and leaving it unable to fund infrastructure improvements.

The Haitian electricity market comprises five isolated areas. Apart from in Port-au-Prince, these are powered by small generators. Electricity production in large cities is largely provided by independent producers, who enjoy monopolies without competition.

There are two policies that could get 24-hour electricity to 50% of the population in 2030, explored by electricity expert Jean Edouard Pauyo. Fixing the transmission network can be compatible with different production technologies, including thermal and renewable energy.

There are two types of electric lines for the transportation of electricity. Transmission lines are high voltage, and carry electricity long distances. Distribution lines are lower voltage and are for short distances, to transport electricity locally. You can see them on the side of the street.

Pauyo has studied the costs and benefits to Haiti of setting up a transmission network, and a distribution network.

A National Transmission Network would connect Port-au-Prince, Jacmel, Jérémie, Gonaïves, Cap-Haïtien, Môle Saint Nicolas, Fort Liberté and the Péligre plant. It would require the construction of approximately 1,079 km of high-voltage power lines connecting the country's main cities, the extension of 12 substations across the country, and the construction of a national energy control center.

The lines would be the most expensive component, costing more than 69 billion gourdes (US$1 billion). The overall investment to build the network would be around 110 billion gourdes (US$1.6 billion). With the ongoing costs for maintaining the transmission network, the total cost across the next three decades will land at 144 billion gourdes (US$2 billion).

But there are significant benefits. This network would help create the conditions for a competitive wholesale electricity market. It will lower the production cost of electricity. It will enable the integration of cleaner renewable energy sources, such as solar and wind turbines. It will lower the cost of rural electrification, thanks to a high voltage network across the country integrating the isolated systems. It will alleviate poverty. And it will lower the steep price that the Haitian economy pays when it cannot currently get electricity to where it is needed. Pauyo estimates these benefits to add up to around 891 billion gourdes (US$13 billion).

What this means is that every gourde spent on creating an integrated electricity transmission network would generate returns to society worth around 6 gourdes.

Setting up a distribution network involves fixing 1,920 km of medium voltage and low voltage lines, constructing 1,350 km of medium and low voltage lines, connecting around 750,000 new subscribers with electronic meters that can be read remotely, and updating the billing system.

Perhaps surprisingly, it is this last task – updating the billing system – that is most expensive part of the investment, at around 6.9 billion gourdes (US$100 million), making up about half of the overall set-up cost of 15.7 billion gourdes (US$228 million). With operations and management and with transmission losses, the total cost over the next thirty years runs to 45 billion gourdes (US$657 million).

Benefits, too, are similar to the transmission network. The distribution network will help increase the rate of access to electricity from 25% to more than 50% of the population. It will allow for the reduction of theft and it will reduce the costs of electricity production. It will help to reduce the costs of breakdowns and improve the living conditions of the population. And it will lead to economic growth.

These benefits to Haiti add up to around 829 billion gourdes (US$6.6 billion). So, each gourde will deliver 10 gourdes of benefit.

There is a compelling case to solve Haiti's electricity problems. Regardless of what steps are taken on production, it is necessary to improve transmission and distribution. The sums involved are large for Haiti – but so, too, are the benefits.

Intervention	Benefit	Cost	BCR
National Transmission Network	891 billion gourdes (US$12.9 billion)	138 billion gourdes (US$2.0 billion)	6
Distribution Networks	449 billion gourdes (US$6.5 billion)	45 billion gourdes (US$660 million)	60

All figures use a discount rate of 5%.

TACKLING ONE-TENTH OF
HAITIAN DEATHS AND
HELPING THE ENVIRONMENT

It sounds almost too good to be true: a single development investment that tackles one of Haiti's biggest death-tolls and at the same time combats deforestation and pollution.

While some research shows Haiti to be almost entirely deforested, recent work finds that up to one-third of land is covered in trees. In any case, having more trees can help Haiti, because it can prevent erosion, aid pollination, and improve water-flow.

In one study, Ruolz Ariste, researcher at Laval University and UQO, explores how to change land management practices to protect more trees.

In optimal agro-silviculture, trees such as moringa are grown around pasture or crops like peanuts. Targeting 257,000 smallholder farmers on 252,000 hectares would mean an additional 9.2% of forest coverage. In addition to the environmental benefits of greater biodiversity, improved waterflow, and reduced erosion, smallholders gain more income from selling leaves, seeds and timber, and nutritional benefits from crop diversification.

The costs, including labor, would add up to about 130,000 HTG per hectare for the first year and nearly 95,000 HTG per hectare subsequently. Should Haiti pursue this policy, each gourde would generate 3 gourdes of social value – a healthy return on investment.

Investment in carbon pricing infrastructure is a synergistic intervention that has the benefit of helping local farmers and the climate.

Internationally, companies that emit carbon can purchase 'offsets' – effectively funding projects reducing greenhouse gas emissions, such as newly forested land in Haiti.

It sounds like a neat way of creating value out of nothing, but there are costs to set up documentation, processes and regulations. Arista calculates that targeting 256,000 smallholder farmers on 251,000 hectares of savanna and rocky bare lands would (without including the private costs) cost 1.55 billion HTG in the first year and 1.04 billion annually after that. There is limited data, but it appears every gourde spent would achieve 1.4 gourdes of benefits.

We can also tackle deforestation by reducing demand for forests to be felled. Between 70% and 95% of the energy used for cooking in Haiti comes from wood and charcoal.

Ariste considers an ambitious plan of biogas scale up which would see 100 biogas plants set up, producing 350 million cubic meters of natural gas, reaching 397,000 households, leading to a reduction of up to 380,000 tons of charcoal. While benefits would be around twice the costs, high initial set-up costs of 78.7 billion HTG could be a deterrent.

There are alternative ways to reduce demand for wood and charcoal, and this is where the prospect of a 'win-win' policy of environmental and health benefits enters the picture.

The vast majority of Haiti cooks with solid fuels, evenly split between wood and charcoal. Nearly half cooks outdoors, more than one-third in a separate building, and 15% in the house.

The resulting air pollution is a silent killer. According to new analysis by environmental economist Bjorn Larsen, this was responsible for 8,200 deaths in Haiti last year. That is one death in ten, making it the fourth most serious health risk factor after malnutrition, unsafe sex, and high blood pressure.

The reason this killer does not have a higher priority is that air pollution quietly leads to heart disease, strokes and lung cancer among adults, and respiratory infections in young children.

Larsen finds that replacing the cookstoves that cause this pollution – and lead to forests being felled for charcoal and wood – would have benefits to Haiti worth 1.3 to 3.9-times the costs, depending on what type of stoves are used.

The cheapest option is Improved Cookstoves – basically, cleaner versions of the charcoal and wood-powered stoves used by Haitians today. While the benefits of just improving the status quo are relatively limited, the cost is as little as $10 or 650 gourdes: that cheap price-tag means this is the most effective of all the solutions explored today, with almost 4 gourdes of benefits for each gourde spent.

While cooking with LPG or ethanol is much more expensive, the health benefits are 1.3 to 2.2 times higher, and thus this is the only real longer-term solution.

More than 4,150 deaths could be avoided annually by full adoption of LPG or ethanol. Non-health benefits include a reduction in wood collection time and fuelwood savings as high as 6000 HTG per year for some households that switch to LPG or ethanol.

But large-scale roll-out of cleaner cookstoves has had very limited success so far. A big factor is monetary: the high initial cost of the stoves and of LPG and ethanol fuel.

Another is that new stoves might not match Haitian cooking preferences. So, while such an intervention has relatively high returns, any policy designed to promote cleaner cookstoves needs to get the local context right – and involve community participation.

Intervention	Benefit	Cost	BCR
Better agroforestry	960 billion gourdes (US$12.9 billion)	320 billion gourdes (US$2.0 billion)	3.0
Carbon pricing infrastructure	52 billion gourdes (US$6.5 billion)	40 billion gourdes (US$660 million)	1.3
Biogas scale-up	290 billion gourdes (US$6.5 billion)	130 billion gourdes (US$660 million)	2.2
Promote improved wood stoves	3,500 gourdes (US$54) per household per year	910 gourdes (US$14) per household per year	3.9
LPG and ethanol stoves for households currently cooking with wood	8,800 gourdes (US$140) per household per year	6,900 gourdes (US$107) per household per year	1.3
LPG and ethanol stoves for households currently cooking with charcoal	15,000 gourdes (US$230) per household per year	6,900 gourdes (US$107) per household per year	2.2

All figures use a discount rate of 5%.

HOW INCREASED ACCESS TO FAMILY PLANNING CAN HELP HAITI

During the 1970s and 1980s, a successful family planning program with strong private and public sector support helped contribute to a decline in Haiti's fertility rate. Political instability in the 1980s saw the dissolution of the National Family Planning Council, the termination of the family planning outreach project, and support for many sexual and reproductive health services shifted to international organizations.

In addition, in the early 1980s, the first cases of HIV infection were diagnosed in Haiti, and by the late 1980s, HIV/AIDS-related funding had overtaken family planning funding, as the government and NGO partners struggled to contain the rapidly-growing epidemic.

While improvements have occurred more recently, political upheavals and economic weakness have continued to affect efforts to improve reproductive health and family planning. As a result, Haiti has fallen behind other countries in sexual and reproductive health services.

The 2010 earthquake and its aftermath severely impacted the entire health system, including sexual and reproductive health. Although there were efforts within days to provide family planning services, there is evidence that the earthquake had significant negative consequences, including on the use of injectables, the most widely used modern contraceptive method in Haiti. The earthquake also negatively affected partnership dynamics such as women's ability to negotiate condom use.

In response, Haiti has worked to revive its family planning program. A 2013 policy states that the provision of free family planning services is required in all health institutions, including workplace infirmaries. In addition, health providers are required to encourage women with more than two or three children to consider a long-acting contraceptive method, and various family planning education and media programs have been devised and implemented. The National Strategic Plan for Reproductive Health and Family Planning for 2013-16 has integrated family planning as a central component in reducing maternal and neonatal mortality.

Haiti is thus hoping to recreate some of its past success, both in reducing fertility and in generating the individual, social and economic benefits that would stem from improved sexual and reproductive health. Professor Hans-Peter Kohler of the University of Pennsylvania has studied the benefits and costs of investing in family planning programs.

The "unmet need" for family planning in Haiti is estimated at 35% – one of the highest rates in the world. This means that more than three women in ten who are sexually active are not using any contraception even though they do not want any more children, or want to delay the next child.

Professor Kohler estimates that expanding sexual and reproductive health services to meet 100% of unmet need would cost 1,496 gourdes per woman, or 1,543 million gourdes annually.

Recent studies found that family planning programs – besides reducing fertility and maternal and child mortality – are likely to result in higher levels of female education, improvements in women's general health, increases in female labor force participation and earnings, and increased child health.

Expanded sexual and reproductive health services would primarily affect the number of years between siblings – and thus, under-five mortality. Under-5 mortality is 145 per 1000 live births for children born within less than 2 years of the previous child, as compared to 102 deaths per 1000 live births for children born within 2 years of the prior birth. The researchers estimate that under-5 mortality would be cut by 70%. Maternal mortality would also be reduced because of fewer births and abortions.

There would also be a 'demographic dividend'. With more access to sexual and reproductive health services, there will be fewer children, and hence relatively more people in the working age. That means Haiti will become slightly more productive: it would increase per capita economic growth by .25 percentage points. Professor Kohler projects that Haiti would be 59 billion gourdes better off annually by 2050 as a result.

Taking these benefits into account, every gourde spent on expanding sexual reproductive health services would generate benefits worth 18 gourdes.

There are additional benefits that were not considered, such as contributions to reducing HIV infections, which would further increase the benefits.

Focusing on restoring past progress on sexual and reproductive health would thus seem to be a very good idea for Haiti.

Intervention	Benefit	Cost	BCR
Access to Contraception	3,600 billion gourdes (US$56 billion)	200 billion gourdes (US$3.1 billion)	18

All figures use a discount rate of 5%.

PUTTING GIRLS' EDUCATION FIRST

The education system is characterized by high costs and unequal distribution of schools, which have an impact on all of Haiti. But rural girls are disproportionately affected.

Girls' education is one of the most powerful things that any nation can invest in, because it creates large and lasting social and economic benefits. Girls who are well-educated go on to lead more empowered, prosperous lives. They delay pregnancy until they are older, affecting maternal and infant mortality rates. And they raise healthier children, creating a virtuous cycle with inter-generational benefits.

Globally, if all girls completed primary school, the number of maternal deaths would be cut by two-thirds, the number of child marriages would drop by 14%, infant mortality would fall by 15%, and 1.7 million children would avoid the stunting of malnutrition.

There are international examples of how to invest in girls' schooling to target those most in need. Some countries have set up scholarships for underprivileged girls. In Bangladesh, rural girls can receive a scholarship if they go to school regularly, get good marks and do not get married during school. This has led to enrolment rates for girls and boys becoming equivalent. Brazil, Kenya and Nicaragua have also achieved promising results with scholarship programs.

Economist-Planner and Project Analyst in the Public Investment Department, Ministry of Planning and External Cooperation (MPCE), Mélissa Torchenaud has written a new research paper that investigates the costs and benefits of setting up a Haitian girls' scholarship scheme.

Across the country, girls and poorer children have higher drop-out rates. In rural areas, this is more pronounced: the attendance rate for extremely poor children is 50% compared to 59% for the Metropolitan Area, and girls in rural areas have lower retention (close to 50%) than those in the Metropolitan area (close to 70%).

Torchenaud's proposed Haiti Girls' Scholarship program would take place over a period of 10 years. During this period, the Ministère de l'Éducation Nationale et de la Formation Professionnelle (MENFP) would pay tuition, two meals a day, and the supply of teaching materials to a group of rural girls admitted in secondary 1 until the end of their traditional studies – a period of 4 years for each girl.

To stay in the scholarship, beneficiaries must have a general average greater than or equal to 60 out of 100 for the fundamental level, and attend school for at least 80% of the academic year.

The main beneficiaries will be girls aged 15-19 who, having completed the 3rd cycle of the basic level, are admitted to Secondary 1, traditionally called 3ème secondaire.

Torchenaud examines the proposal using cost-benefit analysis – a research method that allows the comparison of social, environmental, and health costs and benefits of contrasting policy options. The average cost for each scholarship, per year, would be around 29,782 gourdes for things like tuition, uniforms, and teaching materials. Torchenaud considers the fact that the girls who stay in school could otherwise have tried to get a job, with about one-third succeeding. On average this means they forgo about 28,000 gourdes in income. Including this 'lost' income and some program costs, the total cost per year runs to 67,236 gourdes per student. The total cost to reach 6,583 girls over 4 years would be 1.7 billion gourdes.

The benefits are numerous. For each girl, the wage increase from each additional year of schooling will add up to 262,000 gourdes across her lifetime. As the girl gets one year more education, the risk of her children dying early declines by almost 10%. This alone is worth an extra 61,000 gourdes. More benefits will accrue because more education will decrease the risk of HIV infection, teen pregnancy and maternal mortality rates. It will also improve the nutrition in the next generation of children.

Adding up all such health and economic benefits, the total benefit Haitian society from giving one girl an extra year of schooling is 346,671 gourdes.

About 15 percent of recipients would have stayed in school anyway, and around one in ten will drop out. Accounting for these factors, every Gourde spent on improving girls' school retention through a scholarship for rural girls would have benefits worth 4.4 times more.

49

While it has high returns to Haiti, this scholarship program would only respond to one aspect of the challenges facing Haitian education. Other chapters look at how to improve primary schooling more generally, as well as pre-school education. And of course, there are many other challenges – from energy to health to infrastructure – competing for the same resources.

But this research definitely makes a strong argument for prioritizing keeping girls in school.

Intervention	Benefit	Cost	BCR
Scholarship to improve girls' school retention	7.8 billion gourdes (US$120 million)	1.8 billion gourdes (US$30 million)	4.4

All figures use a discount rate of 5%.

HEALTH IN HAITI:
LESSENING WIDESPREAD DISEASE

HIV/AIDS is the third-biggest cause of death in Haiti. There have been significant breakthroughs over the past decade, with the rate of new HIV infections falling by 54%. More than half of Haitians living with HIV now access live-saving antiretroviral therapy. However, the sustainability of these investments is challenging, because total expenditure on HIV/AIDS is almost exclusively funded from abroad, and the total amount spent exceeds the national health budget.

With colleagues, Karin Stenberg, a health economist at the World Health Organization, carefully examines different proposals for Haiti.

Successful HIV treatment is as effective as consistent condom use in limiting transmission, so scaling up HIV treatment to 80% would save around 20,000 lives, and reaching 95% would save 35,000 lives. This would stop more than 6000 new infections.

The challenge is that treatment remains expensive. However, the evidence from Dr. Stenberg is very clear. Her finding that every gourde spent on test-and-treatment will have benefits worth 3.1 gourdes certainly adds to the armory of advocacy groups arguing for an expansion in treatment.

While HIV has been part of the Haitian landscape for a generation, cholera was only recently introduced. In the short time since 2010, hundreds of thousands of people have been infected, and nearly 10,000 have died. Along with co-authors, Professor Dale Whittington of the University of North Carolina at Chapel Hill and the Manchester Business School has examined vaccination options: should Haiti focus on a school-based or a mass campaign, and should people get one dose or two doses?

Most of us would suggest that the most people should get the highest number of doses. Indeed, this is the way to ensure the broadest possible protection of the population. But Professor Whittington finds that the first vaccine dose makes a lot more difference than the second. What this could suggest to policy-makers is that, if resources are limited, there is more value to use the second vaccine dose on another person.

In economics language, one gourde spent on a mass vaccination with two doses would have benefits worth just over two gourdes, whereas delivering one dose through schools would have benefits worth six gourdes.

Communicable diseases get a lot of attention, but non-communicable disease account for half of all deaths in Haiti. Dr. Ryan McBain, Director of Economic Evaluation at Partners in Health, along with co-authors, looks at three proposals to reduce this death-toll.

High systolic blood pressure, a primary risk factor for stroke and ischemic heart disease events, causes 17.8 percent of all deaths in Haiti. About half of Port-au-Prince residents are hypertensive.

Dr. McBain proposes addressing this through a mass media campaign to educate people to reduce dietary salt intake, and mitigate other factors. This campaign will motivate people to get tested, and encourage a full treatment schedule. The annual costs would be 675 million gourdes (US$9.9 million). The biggest component is the visits to the local health clinics, followed by diagnostic tests. This is expected to avert 520 strokes and 495 heart attacks per year, meaning benefits worth 1.17 billion gourdes (US$17.2 million). Every gourde would achieve nearly 2 gourdes of benefits.

The second proposal is enhanced identification and treatment of children with type-1 diabetes. Partners in Health clinicians in Haiti estimate that only 10-15 percent of the estimated 3,952 Haitian children under age 15 who have type-1 diabetes have access to insulin. This makes their medical outcomes bleak. The annual cost would be 300 million gourdes (US$4.4 million), with 506 lives saved. In economic terms, the benefits are worth 3.6 gourdes for every gourde spent.

Finally, Dr. McBain studies providing teenage girls with a Human Papilloma Virus (HPV) vaccination to prevent cervical cancer. The two most common HPV types are associated with 73 percent of all cervical cancer cases worldwide. In Haiti, at any given time, about one-third of the female population has HPV. Vaccinating 93,000 girls each year is very expensive, however, and every gourde spent on this proposal would have benefits worth just 0.8 of a gourde.

The death-toll of HIV, Cholera, and non-communicable diseases represents a burden on progress, as well as untold misery for many thousands of Haitian families. Only by studying the most effective responses can resources be focused to achieve the most possible.

Intervention	Benefit	Cost	BCR
Cholera Mass Vaccination with Two Doses	54 gourdes (US$0.80) per household per month	26 gourdes (US$0.38) per household per month	2.1
Cholera Mass Vaccination with One Dose	45 gourdes (US$0.66) per household per month	13 gourdes (US$0.19) per household per month	3.5
Cholera School Vaccination with Two Doses	27 gourdes (US$0.39) per household per month	6 gourdes (US$0.09) per household per month	4.5
Cholera School Vaccination with One Dose	18 gourdes (US$0.26) per household per month	3 gourdes (US$0.04) per household per month	5.9
HIV test and treatment	36.67 billion gourdes (US$538 million)	11.74 billion gourdes S$172 million)	3.1
Hypertension	1.17 billion gourdes (US$17.2 million)	675 million gourdes (US$9.9 million)	1.7
Diabetes	1.07 billion gourdes (US$15.7 million)	300 million gourdes (US$4.4 million)	3.6
Cervical Cancer	525 million gourdes (US$7.7 million)	668 million gourdes (US$9.8 million)	0.8

All figures use a discount rate of 5%.

IMMUNIZATION: HOW TO SAVE 16,000 CHILDREN'S LIVES

The Ministry of Public Health and Population, in collaboration with local and international organizations, has made great strides in reducing the infant mortality rate, leading to a decrease from 80 deaths per thousand live births in 2000 to 59 deaths per thousand.

However, Haiti still has the highest infant mortality rate in the Caribbean.

Fewer than half of all children receive every immunization dose. Around two child deaths in ten are caused by diseases that could be prevented by vaccines. These include diphtheria and pertussis.

The biggest causes of vaccine-preventable death are measles and neonatal tetanus. Measles spreads through the air when an infected person coughs or sneezes and is so contagious that if one person has it, 90% of people close by will also become infected if they are not protected.

Tetanus – caused by common bacteria in the soil coming into contact with open cuts – can cause a quick and painful death in very young children, and can also claim the lives of mothers.

Ministry of Planning and External Cooperation (MPCE) economist Magdine Flore Rozier Baldé has researched the benefits of amplifying the MSPP's current efforts, to lift infant immunization coverage to 90% by 2020.

Reasons for Haiti's low immunization coverage include the remoteness and poor quality of health centers, the lack of availability of immunization, and the lack of skilled health personnel.

Of the 644 health institutions providing infant immunization services, an evaluation found that only 264 institutions had personnel that had been trained in the Expanded Program on Immunization, the World Health Organization program that provides national governments with guidelines on immunization coverage.

Therefore, Rozier Baldé suggests focusing on the development of qualified personnel, as well as improving the availability of the basic amenities needed to ensure the quality of immunization. All health institutions in the country that provide immunization services will be strengthened with this investment.

The idea is that this intervention will allow the national immunization coverage rate to rise gradually to 60% in 2017; 70% in 2018; 80% in 2019; and reach 90% by 2020 and 2021.

The cost of vaccination for each child to the government would be around 5,300 gourdes, or USD$78. The total cost of the five-year program would be 2.4 billion gourdes. The bulk of this is the price of immunization and injection equipment, with transportation and training accounting for the rest.

In the first year, an additional 78,624 infants under the age of one would be immunized, and in the second, this would climb to nearly 131,094. Over the course of five years, 864,846 additional children would be immunized, who would otherwise have missed out.

Lives would be saved from the very first year: 975 child deaths would be averted in 2017, and 1,803 in the following year. As the immunization coverage expands, the number would continue to climb until, by the end of the five years, Rozier Baldé finds that 16,506 children would be alive who would otherwise die.

This is a very strong return on a 2.4 billion Gourde investment.

Of course, by saving lives, the intervention will save families a lot of heartbreak. And by avoiding 16,506 children losing almost 70 years of life each, it will have economic benefits. Typically, each year of life that is gained is valued at three-times GDP.

When a child becomes sick, parents understandably miss work. Rozier Baldé estimates that immunization will save parents around 282 million gourdes worth of income that they would otherwise lose.

And it will save the health system nearly 16 million gourdes that would need to be spent on sick children.

Overall, these benefits add up to more than 32.3 billion gourdes. That means that every gourde spent on achieving full immunization for infants will have returns to society worth thirteen gourdes.

Another approach to child health is to provide the nation's 125 municipal regions with a Community Health Center (CCS). The objective would be to improve the provision and quality of services in rural areas and to make the CCS the gateway in the system for these communities. The CCS would deliver promotional, prevention and curative activities, including prenatal and newborn care.

This is the focus of research by Stanley Jean-Baptiste, Planner and Economist at the Ministry of Public Health and Population.

There are different approaches. One is to set up mobile clinics at small or large schools, with school busses delivering nurses and a physician. Fixed clinics at schools would have doctors visit, and nurses on site during school days.

By increasing on its recent successes in expanding infant immunization coverage, and delivering child health initiatives to children at school, Haiti could save tens of thousands of lives.

Intervention	Benefit	Cost	BCR
Full immunization for infants 0-1 years old	32 billion gourdes (US$500 million)	2.4 billion gourdes (US$40 million)	13
Implementation of CCS	3.0 billion gourdes (US$50 million)	770 million gourdes (US$12 million)	4
Small-scale mobile clinic	400 million gourdes (US$6.2 million)	85 million gourdes (US$1.3 million)	4.7
Large-scale mobile clinic	2.0 billion gourdes (US$30 million)	360 million gourdes (US$5.6 million)	5.6
Permanent clinics at schools	2.0 billion gourdes (US$30 million)	520 million gourdes (US$8 million)	3.9

All figures use a discount rate of 5%.

JUSTICE FOR ALL: REDUCING PREVENTIVE DETENTION

All Haitians are equal before the law. So, says the Haitian Constitution. But, access to justice can happen at different speeds for different people.

One reason is the lack of judges. During 2014-2015, there were just 63 trial judges for 8,046 people awaiting trial. Added to this fact, there is a lack of resources to properly operate the judicial and the prison systems. And, according to testimonies and expressions of public sentiment, corruption affects all levels of the judicial system.

But a big factor is affordability. Around sixty percent of the Haitian population do not earn enough to afford representation by a legal professional in a matter of private or public law.

Jimmy Verne, Planner-economist for the Ministry of Planning and External Cooperation (MPCE) has analyzed this situation.

One serious consequence he examines is the state's use of preventive pretrial detention. A study by the National Human Rights Defense Network (RNDDH) in October 2010 revealed that 75% of inmates were in pretrial detention. Five years later, in 2015, the rate had decreased very little (72.19%) according to the Section of Human Rights (SDH) of MINUSTAH.

This causes gross injustices. There are inmates who have already spent two or three years in jail awaiting judgment, for offences for which they would only be sentenced to six months in prison if found guilty.

Verne proposes an expansion of the first Legal Assistance Office program, which officially launched in 2012. The project, which would partner with the Ministry of Justice and Public Security (MJSP) and the Federation of Bar Associations of Haiti, would increase the coverage of the nine Legal Assistance Offices. Currently, the offices cover five of the nation's eighteen first instance courts.

Based on the 2015 prison population, there are more than 7,600 individuals in preventive pretrial detention. Since there are many other factors contributing to this problem, Verne assumes that the investment will reduce the number of cases of preventive pretrial detention by 30%, allowing nearly 2,800 of these detainees to be tried.

It costs 10.7 million gourdes (US$161,000) in set-up costs and remuneration for each office. So, the total budget required would be 139 million gourdes (US$2 million).

There are benefits to detainees and their families. When an individual is released because of this intervention (either because he was not guilty, or because he had already served the sentence for the offence committed), he regains the opportunity to become employed. Those found innocent avoid an average incarceration of 24 months – meaning that over these two years, this group could avoid a loss of around 94 million gourdes (US$1.3 million) in income. For those found guilty, the average sentence is 12 months. Avoiding an additional year incarcerated will mean employment income of 103 million gourdes (US$1.4 million).

But there are also benefits for Haiti as a whole. Detainees are the responsibility of the State. When the State releases individuals from an unjust imprisonment, it also saves the State money. Verne calculates the total savings to be in the order of 82 million gourdes (US$1.1 million).

Added together, one year of a national legal aid program would see benefits to Haitian society worth 390 million gourdes (US$5.3 million).

What this means is that every gourde spent on establishing a nationwide legal aid system would create benefits to society worth 2.8 gourdes.

When we think of ways to support Haiti's progress and development, we often think first of education and health. Those who are in jail may not be the first people we think of. But making sure Haitians are not imprisoned when they shouldn't be is not only economically efficient; it is also just.

Intervention	Benefit	Cost	BCR
Establishment of a national legal aid system	390 million gourdes (US$6.1 million)	140 million gourdes (US$2.2 million)	2.8

All figures use a discount rate of 5%.

REDUCING THE MATERNAL DEATH TOLL

The greatest tragedy about Haiti's rate of maternal mortality – the highest in all of the Americas – is that so many of the deaths are preventable.

In 2013, the maternal mortality ratio or MMR (meaning the number of deaths for every 100,000 live births) was estimated at 380, compared to a regional average of 68.

Progress has been made, but very slowly: In 2015, the MMR was estimated to have reduced to 359, and the neonatal mortality rate (deaths per 1,000 live births) was estimated at 25.4. This is more than double the Sustainable Development Goal target of 12 newborn deaths for every 1,000 live births. And, given these figures, this means that there will be 1,122 maternal deaths and 7,932 newborn deaths in 2017. In Haiti, childbirth too often ends in death. This mustn't be allowed to continue.

The main causes of maternal deaths are severe bleeding, infections, hypertension during pregnancy (pre-eclampsia and eclampsia), and unsafe abortions, while the main causes of newborn deaths include prematurity, asphyxia and sepsis.

One problem is a shortage of skilled caregivers helping at birth. While skilled care at birth increased from 24.2% in 2000 to 37% in 2015, access remains limited and there is a scarcity of trained personnel. Current outputs from midwifery training schools would need to increase by a factor of ten to fulfil the estimated need.

Dr. Karin Stenberg of the World Health Organization and colleagues Ludovic Queuille of the Pan-American Health Organization, Rachel Sanders of Avenir Health, Marcus Cadet of the Ministry of Public Health and Population study ways to reduce the maternal death-toll.

They explore expanding coverage for different packages of interventions. Some of these would be provided during pregnancy, such as routine antenatal care visits, as well as skilled care at birth and immediate postnatal care. Also examined are services provided through emergency obstetric care. This is essential to manage complications and save lives arising at birth. And they look at a package that would ensure that safe abortion and post-abortion care is part of the services provided.

The researchers explore the costs and health benefits for increasing coverage from current levels of these services to reach 95% in 2018, maintaining this coverage until 2036.

The annual additional costs to reach 95% coverage are estimated to range from US$11 million (696 million gourdes) for antenatal care to US$24 million (1,518 million gourdes) for a comprehensive package.

Around 7.7% of health expenditure is estimated to currently be devoted to reproductive health. Expanding access to a comprehensive package would require at least US$1.95 per capita (123.41 gourdes) – or US$135 (123.41 gourdes) per birth. Out of this, the researchers assume US$1.45 (91.80 gourdes) (73%) would be carried by the health sector, and 27% by the education sector. The health sector share is the equivalent of increasing the budget for reproductive health by 41%.

All the packages they examine would save lives, and create returns to society that would be greater than the costs. Put into figures, so that we can compare one policy with another using benefit-cost analysis, we can see that the 'return on investment' for every gourde or dollar invested would be 4 for antenatal care to 18 for a comprehensive combined package.

In absolute numbers of deaths averted however, access to basic and comprehensive emergency obstetric care are the key to mortality reduction.

A comprehensive package for maternal health care – comprising antenatal care, skilled care at birth including management of complications, and access to safe abortion and post abortion care – would avert over 12,000 maternal deaths and close to 74,000 newborn deaths and 25,000 stillbirths during 2018–2036 if made universally available at 95% coverage.

This is equivalent to averting over 650 maternal deaths and close to 3900 newborn deaths and 1300 stillbirths per year.

The maternal mortality ratio would be brought down from its current level of 359 to reach 125 per 100,000 (a reduction by 65%) and the newborn mortality rate would drop from 25 to the Sustainable Development Goal (SDG) target level of 12 per 1,000.

Benefit-cost analysis reveals that such a comprehensive package at 95% coverage would have a benefit-to-cost ratio of 17. This makes reducing the maternal death rates, both financially and morally, an urgent task for Haiti.

Intervention (95% coverage)	Benefit	Cost	BCR
Antenatal care	1,600 billion gourdes (US$25 billion)	440 billion gourdes (US$6.9 billion)	3.6
Skilled assistance for normal delivery	3,800 billion gourdes (US$60 billion)	500 billion gourdes (US$8 billion)	4
Skilled delivery including referral and management of complications	11,000 billion gourdes (US$180 billion)	690 billion gourdes (US$11 billion)	16.2
Combination maternal and newborn health (P1+P3)	12,000 billion gourdes (US$190 billion)	740 billion gourdes (US$12 billion)	16.7
Extended combination package including safe abortion and post abortion care	12,500 billion gourdes (US$198 billion)	740 billion gourdes (US$12 billion)	16.9

All figures use a discount rate of 5%.

SAVINGS LIVES, ONE GOURDE AT A TIME

Along with colleagues, Professor Stephen Vosti of the University of California, Davis has studied micronutrient malnutrition – when the body lacks the necessary vitamins and minerals to thrive. He identifies two different approaches: preventative nutritional investments, and those that treat malnutrition in babies.

Anemia and micronutrient deficiencies affect a large proportion of the population in Haiti. An estimated 21% of children born in the last three years had a low birth weight, although birth weight was reported in only one quarter of births. According to the most recent data, half of women of reproductive age and 65% of preschool children were anemic, or lacking in healthy red blood cells. Anemia in pregnancy is associated with an increased risk of infant mortality, preterm delivery, and low birth weight.

Providing pregnant women with calcium and other micronutrients would reduce the risk of anemia as well as pre-eclampsia or eclampsia, potentially dangerous complications that occur during or after pregnancy.

Each micronutrient tablet costs three gourdes, or even less for calcium alone. Spending 7.6 billion gourdes would avert 15,200 deaths over 12 years, the majority of them newborns. It would prevent 18,800 cases of anemia in pregnant women, and it would make Haitians 80 billion gourdes wealthier, because healthier adults can earn more money. It would mean 120,591 pre-term births would be avoided, and 200,000 newborns would not be of low birth-weight. All told, every gourde spent on this initiative would generate benefits worth 10 gourdes.

Between the ages of 6 and 24 months, Vosti and his coauthors look at another way to help: we can provide young children with micronutrient sachets to prevent anemia and micronutrient deficiencies. A sachet for one day costs just one gourde, and children need sachets for four months each year. This is very cheap, costing just over 157 million gourdes to reach 1.4 million children over 12 years.

Around 417,690 cases of anemia will be averted over 12 years for pre-school aged children. Every gourde spent will generate benefits to Haiti worth 8 gourdes.

However, getting people to take pills or sachets is harder than simply improving the nutrition of the food that they are already eating. Professor Vosti and his colleagues suggest adding iron and folic acid to wheat flour, something that is done around the world. This is known as 'fortification' and, while it is mandatory according to Haitian law, it appears that most flour in Haiti is not fortified with these micronutrients.

Spending just 331 million gourdes on pre-mixed micronutrients, equipment and training, would save 1,300 newborn lives over 12 years, as well as avert 869,000 cases of anemia in women, 562,000 cases of anemia in pre-school aged children, and 927,000 cases of anemia in school-aged children.

These are extraordinarily high benefits for a relatively small investment. Put into monetary terms, each gourde spent would generate benefits worth 24 gourdes.

These three approaches would all aim to prevent the challenges of malnutrition before they occur. But Professor Vosti also examines how to deal with severe and moderate malnutrition in young children, which affect tens of thousands of Haitians every year.

What is required is improving and expanding the screening of malnutrition for children under 5 years of age from the current level of 70 percent to 95 percent, and providing those who need it with a therapeutic food.

This would cost about 1.18 billion gourdes. Of this, one-third would cover the costs of RUTF (ready-to-eat-therapeutic food) products, one-third would cover additional personnel costs, and one-third would cover the costs of transporting children to/from treatment centers. The same formula could be made with local ingredients, which would save about 50 million gourdes.

Today, 70 percent of children suffering from severe malnutrition are treated, along with 25% of those suffering from moderate malnutrition. Those figures would both increase to 95%.

A 12-year intervention will screen an additional 1.7 million children, treat approximately 351,000 additional cases, and save more than 5,700 lives.

The results of every investment in nutrition can be measured in the numbers of lives saved. This research shows that preventing and treating micronutrient malnutrition would be highly effective for Haiti.

Intervention	Benefit	Cost	BCR
Calcium and micronutrients to pregnant women	80 billion gourdes (US$1.2 billion)	7.6 billion gourdes (US$120 million)	10
Wheat flour fortification with iron and folic acid	7.9 billion gourdes (US$120 million)	330 million gourdes (US$5.3 million)	4
Micronutrient powders to children 6-24 months of age	1.2 billion gourdes (US$20 million)	160 million gourdes (US$2.5 million)	16.2
Treat wasting with standard formula RUTF	11 billion gourdes (US$1.7 million)	1.2 billion gourdes (US$20 million)	16.7
Treat wasting with RUTF made locally in Haiti	11 billion gourdes (US$1.7 million)	1.1 billion gourdes (US$20 million)	16.9

All figures use a discount rate of 5%.

IMPROVING LEARNING
IN THE CLASSROOM

In Haiti, about ninety percent of children are estimated to be in primary school. That is a real achievement compared to 20 years ago. But evidence shows that it is not enough to ensure that children are in the classroom. For real benefits, children need to engage in real learning when they are at school.

Improving the quality of education and retention of students to the end of primary school and beyond poses a challenge for Haiti.

In the latest research, Dr. Damien Échevin, Economist and Research Associate at University of Sherbrooke and Laval University, works to identify the costs and benefits of proposals that may improve access, retention and quality.

The first such idea is to provide primary education in Creole rather than French. This has been much-discussed in recent years.

Dr. Échevin estimates that the upfront cost of switching to instruction in Creole is around 22,000 gourdes (US$319) per pupil over the entire length of time they spend in primary school. He projects this would lead to 73% of children completing primary school, an increase from today's 50% rate. Other benefits would include higher future wages for those children from their extra education, and a saving for the education system. These benefits would add up to 182,000 gourdes (US$2,665) per pupil.

This means that every gourde spent would achieve benefits worth 8.4 gourdes. However, there are disadvantages. Although mother tongue instruction would lower dropout rates and increase primary school completion, returns to speaking Creole are limited. There are potential negative effects of having less proficiency in a global language like French. Children would need to learn another language to broaden their economic horizons. And private schools that have French as the official language of instruction may syphon off the wealthier students. The economic analysis adds new information for this debate, and suggests that this proposal warrants further discussion.

Another oft-discussed approach to improving education is to improve teacher training. According to figures from the Ministry of National Education and Vocational Training (MENFP), public and non-public institutions offering in-service initial training for fundamental and secondary teachers are responsible for about 400 graduates every year. This number is insufficient to meet the needs of the education system.

On a per-pupil basis, improved teacher training would cost 8,900 gourdes (US$131) over the entire primary school time. This includes training costs for the teacher and a salary increase. This improvement in teacher training will lead to better education, and thus to higher income for children over their lifetimes. This is worth 54,000 gourdes (US$789) per pupil, meaning that every gourde spent generates benefits worth 6 gourdes.

An alternative approach is to subsidize access to private schools. The supply of public schools in Haiti is limited. According to the 2013–14 school census, only 16% of the 16,993 schools in Haiti are public.

A subsidy could come in the form of a voucher or tuition subsidies. Tuition waiver programs have had a proven impact on participation in Haiti. However, by increasing the ratio of students-to-teacher, such an approach could have a detrimental effect on educational outcomes.

This is substantially more expensive than either of the first two proposals. Funding such a subsidy would cost 48,000 gourdes (US$703) per pupil over the entire primary school. Again, we would see an increase in both future wages as well as completion rates – and this would also save the education system money. Added together, these benefits are worth 139,000 gourdes (US$2,041) per pupil. So, every gourde spent generates benefits for Haiti worth 2.9 gourdes.

Finally, Dr. Échevin considers whether the cost of a school uniform may be posing a barrier to education. The school uniform represents a large share of education expenditure in developing countries and it is generally considered a serious impediment to school enrollment. Data from elsewhere suggests that provision of free school uniforms leads to 10%-15% reductions in dropout rates.

A uniform costs just 3,500 gourdes per student per year, or 18,000 gourdes (US$256) for a pupil for the entire primary school. Dr. Échevin projects that such investment could increase completion rates from

50 to 56 percent [from spreadsheet), increasing the future earnings of children who stay in school longer, and save parents the cost of the uniform. Such benefits add up to 53,000 gourdes (US$778) per pupil. So, every gourde spent leads to 3 gourdes of benefits.

Along with other papers on education, this latest study adds to the evidence base for decision-makers to consider when identifying not only how to improve educational access, but how to keep children in school for longer, to learn more while they are there.

Intervention	Benefit (per primary school child)	Cost (per primary school child)	BCR
Mother tongue instruction	$2,700	$319	8.4
Training teachers	$790	$130	6.0
Private school subsidies	$2,000	$700	2.9
Free uniforms	$780	$250	3.0

All figures use a discount rate of 5%.

A MENU OF OPTIONS TO
IMPROVE PUBLIC SERVICES

Many proposals have been made in the past ten years to make the public sector more effective. Despite these efforts, public services remain in a critical state, illustrated by strikes, delays caused by red tape, and difficulties for citizens to do things like getting a passport, registering land, or clearing customs for imported goods. The improvement of public services continues to pose a challenge for Haiti.

Research by economist Riphard Serent from Quisqueya University and Center for International and Diplomatic Studies focuses on raising public sector performance.

Two options are paying public servants more across-the-board, or introducing performance-based pay.

Increasing salaries by 10% would cost 3.26 billion gourdes annually. However, based on evidence from other countries, Serent concludes that this approach would not generate benefits worth more than the cost.

Performance-based pay would do more. Many studies show that bonuses can increase employees' effort, particularly when output can easily be measured. In a 1999 pilot program in Haiti, performance-based pay increased health coverage and improved health services.

Serent finds that the total cost of introducing performance-based bonuses for certain public sector workers would be 1.34 billion gourdes, and the improvements in productivity would be worth 4.76 billion gourdes.

Another new research paper from Ministry of Planning and External Cooperation economist-planner, Bertrand Joseph focuses on how to solve log-jams in land registration. Haiti has seen an exponential increase in land value, along with major conflicts. Many transactions and land transfers happen informally, and land disputes are difficult for the justice system to resolve.

The registration process is very slow. The General Directorate of Taxes' land register covers 2,500 books. The GDT has digitized part of its archives, but this was done to retain them, but not to streamline the process.

Digitizing and formalizing these records would provoke many dormant ownership conflicts. Joseph estimates there would be around 500,000 conflicts during digitization. Each would cost about 20,000 gourdes for judicial resolution. Added to the cost of computers and salaries, digitization would cost 8.37 billion gourdes annually.

In total, the annual benefits are worth 21.4 billion gourdes. This means every gourde would achieve 2.6 gourdes of benefits.

Using technology to streamline the operations at Cap-Haitien Port would also reduce bureaucratic delays, according to a new research paper by Yvrose Guerrier, department head at the Ministry of Planning and External Cooperation.

Haiti has enormous maritime potential with more than 1,500 kilometers of coastline, but is among the Caribbean countries that exploit their marine resources the least.

Guerrier finds that improved computerization would strengthen the security of Haiti's borders and reduce the cost of port services, as well as improving customs import times. The benefits would add up to 5.25 billion gourdes. Costs, which include acquisition of technology and services, training, salary increases, and maintenance, would amount to 750 million gourdes. This means that every gourde spent would generate benefits to Haiti worth 7.0 gourdes.

The Ministry of Trade and Industry's Director of Studies and Programming, Romy Reggiani Theodat, approaches public services from a different angle in his research paper that focuses on government procurement.

The Haitian government spends about 15% of GDP every year through various public tenders, which foreign firms win more than 70% of the time. This means that a lot of public spending goes abroad, rather than building the local economy. Integration with CARICOM and a likely contract with the World Trade Organization means even more exposure to foreign competition. Haitian companies are at a disadvantage because of their low level of capitalization, high operating costs and low level of technology.

Professor Theodat suggests inserting a clause into public tenders that stipulates that any international business that wins must subcontract 20% of the contract to Haitian businesses.

Doing so would increase the cost of procurement, as well as incurring administrative expenses. Altogether, the price-tag for Haiti would be 13.98 billion gourdes a year.

This would develop Haitian companies' skills and improve their competitiveness. It would make local companies more productive. The benefits would be worth in the region of 62.90 billion gourdes, meaning that every gourde spent on this initiative would generate a 'return on investment' for Haiti worth 4.5 gourdes.

Together, this shows that there are multiple opportunities for Haiti to improve public services, which would improve livelihoods and make the entire nation better off.

Intervention	Benefit	Cost	BCR
Raising public sector salaries	3.3 billion gourdes (US$50 million)	3.3 billion gourdes (US$50 million)	1.0
Performance-based pay program	4.8 billion gourdes (US$70 million)	1.3 billion gourdes (US$20 million)	3.5
Digitize land records	21 billion gourdes (US$330 million)	8.4 billion gourdes (US$130 million)	2.6
Computerization at Cap-Haïtien Port	5.3 billion gourdes (US$80 million)	750 million gourdes (US$12 million)	7.0
Local content procurement	63 billion gourdes (US$980 million)	14 billion gourdes (US$220 million)	4.5

All figures use a discount rate of 5%.

THE CASE FOR BUILDING ROADS

Transport problems affect every aspect of life in Haiti. The problems are all too familiar to Haitians. Roads degrade faster than they are rehabilitated or built. The inadequacy of the road network, combined with the pitiful state of roads and transport vehicles, means a large part of the rural population is isolated.

In fact, more than half of these people have no access to transportation, and more than a third rely on roads that are difficult to access. These conditions extremely limit access to basic services and opportunities for economic development.

Amien Sauveur from the Ministry of Planning and External Cooperation (Ministère de la Planification et de la Coopération Externe) has researched responses to the road infrastructure deficit. His paper builds the case for investment in two specific projects.

The Northwest department is the only department in the country that does not have access to a single kilometer of concrete or paved road. Port-de-Paix is connected to no other city except by clay roads. The Northwest is highly vulnerable to weather hazards due to the lack of mitigation work such as drainage and gullies, and stabilization of riverbanks.

This situation, coupled with the progressive degradation of river banks, can make it difficult to access communes including Saint-Louis du Nord, Anse-à-Foleur and Chansolme in the event of disasters.

To this end, Sauveur argues that establishing the Gonaïves road section at Port-de-Paix is of paramount importance.

Working out the costs for the 83km road is fairly straightforward, based on large-scale studies from across the world. Each kilometer of road would cost $300,000 per kilometer in studies, $1.5 million in construction, and $375,000 in maintenance. The total cost would be 16.5 billion gourdes, or $238 million.

The benefits would be manifold. Right now, the average speed of traffic in the area is just 30 kilometers per hour. After the new road is built that will climb to 70 kilometers per hour. People and cargo will move more swiftly. It will save time and money: Sauveur calculates the time-saved for people will be worth 716 million gourdes to the Haitian economy, and for goods it will be worth 11 billion gourdes.

There will be other benefits. Currently, there are around 320 accidents. Sauveur estimates that they will nearly halve, thanks to the new road. Put into monetary terms, this will mean annual savings to Haiti of 7.2 billion gourdes (US$104 million).

And this one stretch of road will mean that more crops can be delivered to consumers without spoiling. That reduction in post-harvest losses is worth another 8 billion gourdes.

Added together, all of the benefits add up to 37 billion gourdes (US$540 million). So, the benefits of building the Gonaïves road is 2.3 times the costs – a respectable investment.

Sauveur's second proposed intervention is a bridge across the River Anglais, linking the department of the South and that of the Grand'Anse.

It is a bridge with a length between 120 to 150 meters, costing around 228 million gourdes (US$3.3 million). The place where vehicles cross the river now is too close to the coast. As a result, 2-to-3 km of roads would also need to be constructed, to move the bridge further from the coast, at a cost of $3.7 million.

The total cost of planning, construction and maintenance would be 883 million gourdes (US$12.7 million).

Similar to the road, the benefits would include saved time for people (worth 30 million gourdes), saved time for cargo (worth 947 million gourdes), and a reduction in vehicle use costs (48 million gourdes). The reduction in post-harvest losses would be worth a large 304 million gourdes. Altogether, these benefits are worth 1.3 billion gourdes (US$19 million). This means that building the bridge over the River Anglais will generate benefits to all of Haiti worth 1.5 times the total costs.

The challenges of poor road infrastructure are well known to Haitians. Research highlighting the benefits helps to build the case for greater investment.

Intervention	Benefit	Cost	BCR
Route Gonaives to P-d-P	37 billion gourdes (US$580 million)	17 billion gourdes (US$260 million)	2.3
Bridge over les Anglais	1.3 billion gourdes (US$20 million)	880 million gourdes (US$14 million)	1.5

All figures use a discount rate of 5%.

WATER AND SANITATION SERVICES: RURAL OR URBAN HAITI FIRST?

Low coverage rates for clean water and sanitation leave Haiti exposed to significant health burdens. According to the latest estimates, 72% of Haiti's population lack access to improved sanitation facilities and use either shared facilities, other improved facilities, or defecate in the open.

In urban areas, 66% of the population lacks access to improved facilities while in rural areas, 81% of the total population lacks access to improved facilities.

Between 2,000 and 4,500 people die each year from diarrheal disease. And the lack of basic water and sanitation services has contributed to the spread of waterborne diseases, including the cholera outbreak introduced by the United Nations in 2010.

Better water and sanitation services would make it harder for such diseases to spread. But here, as in every other policy area, Haiti faces options.

Professor Dale Whittington of the University of North Carolina at Chapel Hill, and two colleagues, explore these options.

The *National Plan for the Elimination of Cholera in Haiti, 2013–2022* specifically calls for interventions to improve water and sanitation conditions across the country and especially in remote rural areas with limited access to healthcare facilities. Many international organizations and NGOs have responded by investing in this sector. However, many rural Haitians continue to live without access to these basic services.

The first option Professor Whittington considers is the use of a borehole and hand-pump. While this system is easy to operate, maintaining it can be a challenge. The upfront financial cost of digging a borehole and setting up a hand-pump is estimated to be 443,000 gourdes (US$6,500) for the parts and installation. An associated education campaign and the establishment of a community management structure – to ensure repairs and community-level management – costs an additional

238,000 gourdes (US$3,500). Therefore, the total upfront cost per borehole and hand-pump is estimated to be 682,000 gourdes (US$10,000).

One system would serve 60 households, so for each household the cost would be 11,000 gourdes (US$167). Adding in maintenance costs, the total costs over the lifetime of the 15 years of the technology, per month, per household, is about 150 gourdes (US$2.20).

In total terms, the benefits would be worth 2.2 gourdes for every 1 gourde spent.

An alternative approach for rural communities is to focus on achieving community-led total sanitation, known as CLTS. This is a behavior change strategy for ending open defecation that attempts to raise awareness among community members of the risks associated with open defecation. The aim is to increase villagers' perceived need to end open defecation and to ensure that every household and individual uses a latrine, thereby achieving "total sanitation." This requires a campaign to get everyone onboard at the community, but it also requires constructing latrines. The upfront financial cost per household for constructing a pit latrine in rural Haiti is estimated to be US$20, plus a monthly US$0.30 program cost per household to cover the expenses of delivering the behavioral intervention, and another US$0.42 per household per month for operations and maintenance – including things like purchasing soap, a pail, or other necessary items to clean or repair a latrine. The total monthly cost, therefore, is $1.10 per household per month. The benefits are both averted health problems and time saved from not having to walk far to defecate – in total about $1.21.

In another paper, Dr. Rachel Sklar of the UC Berkeley School of Public Health studies opportunities to improve urban sanitation. Currently there are 741,000 urban households that lack access.

The first approach she considers would connect a household latrine to a septic tank, emptied by a professional company once every 4.5 years.

The second approach is to use so-called "container-based sanitation", where a household container-based toilet is emptied professionally once per week. The waste is transformed into products like animal feed, fertilizer, or compost. This approach has been gaining traction in urban areas of Kenya, Ghana, Haiti and Peru, where issues like land tenure or lack of available space preclude households from having a safe sanitation system within their homes. Since a container-based toilet requires little modification to the house, it is suitable for tenants and single room dwellings.

The costs of achieving near-total urban sanitation with both methods are roughly comparable. It costs 1.7 billion gourdes in total for the container-based solution, and 1.8 billion gourdes for the pit latrine approach.

Achieving universal sanitation in urban areas for all 3.7 million urban dwellers lacking good sanitation would unlock health, productivity and educational benefits. It would save 254 deaths from diarrhea each year, and avert 796,893 diarrhea cases. Put into financial terms, the deaths avoided are worth 664 million gourdes. Time savings are worth another 434 million gourdes. Other savings include the avoided illness, avoided healthcare costs, and the benefits of children spending more time in school.

Added up, the total benefits for achieving urban sanitation are worth 1.7 billion gourdes. This is similar to the amount that it would cost to deliver a container-based sanitation approach, and slightly lower than the costs of a pit latrine approach.

Of course, in reality politicians and donors tend not to make a stark decision between serving rural or urban populations first – and rightly so. The new research papers do serve a purpose, however, in helping decision-makers fully understand the impacts and effects from approaching water and sanitation issues in different ways.

Intervention	Benefit	Cost	BCR
Borehole and Hand-pump in rural areas	327 gourdes (US$4.79) per household per month	150 gourdes (US$2.17) per household per month	2.2
Community-Led Total Sanitation in rural areas	82 gourdes (US$1.21) per household per month	75 gourdes (US$1.10) per household per month	1.1
Pit Latrines in urban areas for 3.7 million people	1.7 billion gourdes (US$23.5 million)	1.8 billion gourdes (US$26.5 million)	0.9
Container Based Sanitation in urban areas	1.7 billion gourdes (US$23.5 million)	1.7 billion gourdes (US$23.5 million)	1.0

All figures use a discount rate of 5%.

COULD PATERNITY LEAVE HELP
WOMEN EARN MORE?

In Haiti, as in most nations, social distortions and inequalities make it harder for women to participate in the labor market as much as men.

According to a study carried out by the Ministry of Women's Affairs and Rights (MCFDF), women make up less than one-third of the formal sector. In addition to having less access to employment opportunities than men, women work in more precarious jobs and the income they generate remains lower. Women hold less than ten percent of management positions.

How to tackle this problem is the topic of a research by Mélissa Torchenaud, project analyst in the Department of Public Investment of the Ministry of Planning and External Cooperation.

Torchenaud suggests what may seem like an unexpected solution to the challenge of an imbalanced workforce: establishing paternity leave for new fathers.

The idea is that by inviting men to take paid and non-transferable six-week break after the delivery of their child, there will be the opportunity for greater gender equity in the labor market, in particular to improve the participation of women and their access to management functions at all levels of decision-making.

Employers are reluctant to hire women partly because women may be absent for long periods due to maternity. This intervention will undermine that argument, while posing a curb on the almost certain interruption of women's careers after a birth.

Torchenaud anticipates that 90% of fathers' leave will be taken, and the percentage of women working in the formal sector will increase by 6.8% annually; the gender pay gap, currently 32% in Haiti, will be reduced; and free time at home is created for men.

The paternity leave itself will cost 2 billion gourdes, while the employment displacement for men imposes a cost of 71.9 billion gourdes.

The expected benefits are increased employment for women, free time for men and increased productivity for companies that diversify their employee profile.

The benefit of more women remaining in the labor force is of the same magnitude as the cost of employment displacement for men: a decline in the employment of men leads to an increase in the employment of women. This benefit is worth 71.9 billion gourdes. The benefits of free-time for men are the same magnitude as the cost of paternity leave: 2.0 billion.

It has been shown overseas that paid paternity leave leads to a reduction in the pay gap. The resulting increase in productivity for businesses from the increase in women's employment would be worth 23 billion gourdes.

The total benefits for one year are 96.9 billion gourdes. This means that each gourde spent on the paternity leave policy will generate returns to society worth 1.3 gourdes.

While this would lead to benefits for the formal labor market, it would not affect the informal labor market. Domestic workers, the majority of whom are women and children, feel the effects of inequality. In addition to often being paid poorly, they are virtually excluded from labor protection.

Torchenaud studies the effects of a 43% increase in the domestic worker minimum wage set in May 2016 by President Jocelerme Privert. The wage would therefore be 250 gourdes instead of 175 gourdes.

The objective is to improve incomes so that domestic workers can better meet their needs and have better access to basic services.

This would cost 3.7 billion gourdes a year. The cost largely falls to employers, but there are also extra costs for to the education system. When we pay people more, they access more basic services, and in this case, that means schooling for the children of domestic workers.

This extra schooling also delivers one of the benefits of the scheme, namely higher incomes for the children of the domestic servants. Other benefits include a decrease in babies born under-weight because their mothers can afford better food. The biggest benefit though is the increase in wealth to the domestic workers.

But there is a downside. The intervention may lead to job losses.

Standard economic theory tells us that higher wages will lead to lower employment – meaning some domestic servants will lose their jobs entirely after an increase in the minimum wage. However, studies from South Africa actually show that even a substantial rise in the minimum wage of informal workers surprisingly did not reduce the number or hours of employment.

If there were no job losses at all, then every gourde spent on the policy would generate 1.15 gourdes of benefits. But even with a 5.6 percent job loss, the benefits are slightly higher than the costs.

Inequality for women and low wages for domestic workers are important challenges. There are no simple answers, but now we at least know two ways to tackle these problems that do slightly more good for each gourde spent.

Intervention	Benefit	Cost	BCR
Paternity Leave	13 billion gourdes (US$200 million)	9.6 billion gourdes (US$150 million)	1.3
Minimum Wage Increase (with no job loss)	4.3 billion gourdes (US$70 million)	3.4 billion gourdes (US$50 million)	1.2
Minimum Wage Increase (with a 5.57% job loss)	4.1 billion gourdes (US$60 million)	3.8 billion gourdes (US$60 million)	1.1

All figures use a discount rate of 5%.

CRUCIAL PRIORITIES FOR HAITI'S YOUTH

In May 2017, Haiti Priorise invited 9 youth leaders from around the country to deliberate and provide their input on Haiti's top priorities for the coming years. This important input was shared with the Eminent Panel, which included Nobel Laureate Vernon Smith and prominent Haitian economists: Kesner Pharel, Ketleen Florestal, and Raymond Magloire, giving a crucial voice to Haiti's youth.

These young leaders represent 9 of Haiti's departments. They were selected from a pool of more than 400 candidates who attended Haiti Priorise's Regional Youth Forums held in partnership with universities and youth organizations across the country. After deliberating and conducting their own prioritizations of new cost-benefit analysis research of more than 80 policies, the top candidates from each department were invited to Port-au-Prince to kick off the Haiti Priorise Research Conference.

Each of these young men and women comes from a different background. Among them, we have a law student, a biology major, a teacher, and even a TV personality. Despite these differences, they shared similar views on what it would take to do more good and pave the way for a brighter, more prosperous future for Haiti. Some of their top priorities focused on reforming EDH, Haiti's electricity utility company, providing better access to contraception, and offering civic education in the national curriculum to promote more citizen engagement. Together, they believe these policies would help create more opportunities to boost Haiti's social and economic development.

At the Grande Anse Regional Youth Forum, Evodie Jeune, a law student from Jeremie, described the personal devastation that she and her family experienced in the aftermath of Hurricane Matthew. At that youth forum in Jeremie, she went on to describe the numerous challenges people who are displaced face in trying to access the most basic public services several months after the hurricane hit Haiti's southern regions.

Indeed, this is a pressing issue, but so are many others. What should the government and other key stakeholders prioritize in the years ahead? Which policies would generate the most returns per gourde spent? Should the government prioritize decentralization or access to contraception; first responders or the road from Gonaives to Port-de-Paix? These hard decisions make prioritization imperative for Haiti's future. But, despite contrasting experiences, these youth leaders share a common vision for Haiti that is richer, healthier, and more productive.

Haiti Priorise has looked at over 80 solutions, across a number of sectors. Some of the solutions are really good investments, like wheat flour fortification to save lives and avoid anemia, or early childhood stimulation which has wide-spanning benefits that follow the children the rest of their lives. Others, such as imposing a tariff on imported rice and HPV vaccines, have costs that outweigh the benefits, making them bad investments.

The Haitian youth accounts for over half of Haiti's population, but is usually absent from discussions about the country's future. Haiti Priorise, using the analysis provided by economist researchers, from Haiti and abroad, traveled throughout the country to get young people to participate in debates and discussions about the best solutions to the most pressing problems affecting different regions throughout Haiti.

With engaged learning and new research, they identified the most promising solutions to improve the lives of those in their region and throughout the country, essentially identifying more ways to make smarter investments that lead to a richer Haiti and a healthier population.

Summary of the Haiti Priorise Regional Youth Forums

Center Department Regional Youth Forum in Hinche, Haiti

Hosted at Université Notre Dame d'Haiti, Unités Diocésaines de l'Enseignement, de Recherche et de Service (UDERS) de Hinche on February 4, 2017

Haiti Priorise was pleased to welcome 53 youth leaders from the Center Department to participate in a prioritization of policy solutions aimed at addressing some of the key challenges faced in the region.

Highest priorities: civics education, child vaccines 0-1, and urban ambulance network

Lowest priorities: e-voting and graduation program

Kerruly Julsaint, a biology major, represented the Center Department at the Haiti Priorise Research Conference in Port-au-Prince in May 2017.

Nippes Department Regional Youth Forum in Miragoane, Haiti

Hosted at Université Publique des Nippes (UPNIP) on February 18, 2017

Haiti Priorise was pleased to welcome 55 youth leaders from the Nippes Department to participate in a prioritization of policy solutions aimed at addressing some of the key challenges faced in the region.

Highest priorities: civics education, wheat fortification, and first responders

Lowest priority: microfinance program

Roberno Richard, a sociology major, represented the Nippes Department at the Haiti Priorise Research Conference in Port-au-Prince in May 2017.

Northeast Department Regional Youth Forum in Fort- Liberté, Haiti

Hosted at Université d'Etat d'Haiti, Ecole de Droit et de la Science Economique de Fort-Liberté on February 24, 2017

Haiti Priorise was pleased to welcome 51 youth leaders from the Northeast Department to participate in a prioritization of policy solutions aimed at addressing some of the key challenges faced in the region.

Highest priorities: civics education and decentralization

Lowest priority: national ambulance network

Bethania Michel, an education major, represented the Northeast Department at the Haiti Priorise Research Conference in Port-au-Prince in May 2017.

Northwest Department Regional Youth Forum in Port-de-Paix, Haiti

Hosted at Université Valparaiso on March 11, 2017

Haiti Priorise was pleased to welcome 48 youth leaders from the Northwest Department to participate in a prioritization of policy solutions aimed at addressing some of the key challenges faced in the region.

Highest priorities: civics education, wheat fortification, and urban ambulance network

Lowest priority: graduation program

Sonet Thema, an education major, represented the Northwest Department at the Haiti Priorise Research Conference in Port-au-Prince in May 2017.

South Department Regional Youth Forum in Les Cayes, Haiti

Hosted at American University of the Caribbean on March 17 2017

Haiti Priorise was pleased to welcome 63 youth leaders from the South Department to participate in a prioritization of policy solutions aimed at addressing some of the key challenges faced in the region.

Highest priorities: civics education and hypertension screening and treatment

Lowest priority: graduation program

Zachary Gedeon, a civil engineering major, represented the South Department at the Haiti Priorise Research Conference in Port-au-Prince in May 2017.

Southeast Department Regional Youth Forum in Jacmel, Haiti

Hosted at Université Notre Dame d'Haiti, UDERS de Jacmel on March 25, 2017

Haiti Priorise was pleased to welcome 40 youth leaders from the Southeast Department to participate in a prioritization of policy solutions aimed at addressing some of the key challenges faced in the region.

Highest priorities: civics education, child vaccines 0-1, and first responders

Lowest priority: graduation program

Dieucile Adonis, a nursing major, represented the Southeast Department at the Haiti Priorise Research Conference in Port-au-Prince in May 2017.

Grande Anse Department Regional Youth Forum in Jeremie, Haiti

Hosted at Bibliotheque Diocesaine Carl Edward Peters de Jeremie on April 1, 2017

Haiti Priorise was pleased to welcome 50 youth leaders from the Grande Anse Department to participate in a prioritization of policy solutions aimed at addressing some of the key challenges faced in the region.

Highest priorities: civics education, first responders, and decentralization

Lowest priority: microfinance program

Evodie Jeune, a law student, represented the Grande Anse Department at the Haiti Priorise Research Conference in Port-au-Prince in May 2017.

North Department Regional Youth Forum in Limonade, Haiti

Hosted at Université d'Etat d'Haiti, Campus Roi Henry de Limonade on April 7, 2017

Haiti Priorise was pleased to welcome 65 youth leaders from the North Department to participate in a prioritization of policy solutions aimed at addressing some of the key challenges faced in the region.

Highest priorities: civics education and decentralization

Lowest priority: graduation program

Gregory Clervaux, a sociology major, represented the North Department at the Haiti Priorise Research Conference in Port-au-Prince in May 2017.

Artibonite Department Regional Youth Forum in Gonaives, Haiti

Hosted at Université Notre Dame d'Haiti, UDERS de Gonaives on April 8, 2017

Haiti Priorise was pleased to welcome 48 youth leaders from the Artibonite Department to participate in a prioritization of policy solutions aimed at addressing some of the key challenges faced in the region.

Highest priorities: civics education, decentralization, and urban ambulance network

Lowest priority: graduation program

Ruben Daminthas, a business major, represented the Artibonite Department at the Haiti Priorise Research Conference in Port-au-Prince in May 2017.

Intervention	Benefit Cost Ratio (BCR)
Reform Electricity Utility	22
Access to Contraception	18
Civic Education for Youth	5
Train First Responders	16
Expand Mobile Broadband	12
Road Gonaives to P-De-Px	2
Better Agroforestry	3
Rural Borehole and Handpump	2
Electronic Registration of Birth Certificate	11
Decentralized Government	10
Shelters and Early Warning System For Floods	4

The list is not a ranking of policies by Haitian youth. This is a list of policy interventions selected from more than 80 interventions researched using cost-benefit analysis for the Haiti Priorise project.

CONCLUSION

Like every nation, Haiti has limited resources. Prioritization is needed. Understanding the costs and benefits of different policies and proposals can help decision-makers to focus on the most effective investments.

In this book, we have shared the research from *Haiti Priorise*. This has been written by more than 50 economists from Haiti and abroad, who studied 85 concrete proposals that would improve the nation's well-being.

After completing the research found in this book, these researchers presented all of their findings to an Eminent Panel of distinguished economists in Port-au-Prince. This panel comprised Ketleen Florestal (advisor to the Executive Directors of Haiti at the World Bank Group and the International Monetary Fund), Philomé Joseph Raymond Magloire (former governor of the Central Bank), Kesner Pharel (renowned Haitian economist and economics commentator), and Vernon Smith (Nobel laureate economist).

The Eminent Panel interviewed the researchers and deliberated, before agreeing on a list of the most effective investments for Haiti. As Vernon Smith said, "such knowledge is sorely needed for informed decisions to be made on any nation's future."

For that reason, the findings were also presented by the distinguished economists to President Jovenel Moïse, Prime Minister Jack Guy Lafontant, President of the Senate Youri Latortue, and other Cabinet members including the Minister of Planification and External Cooperation, Aviol Fleurant, and to MPCE technicians.

However, as Ketleen Florestal said, "the research and findings of Haiti Priorise make very useful reading not just for the government, but for donors and NGOs – and to anyone with an interest in this nation's future."

In that spirit, we are sharing with readers the top priorities identified by Haiti Priorise.

It is important to make the point that the Eminent Panel studied and prioritized specific proposals, and not challenges, while noting that resolving challenges including reducing domestic violence and raising wages (especially for women) is important for Haiti.

With these important caveats noted, the Eminent Panel's findings offer considerable insight into policies and actions that would achieve huge benefits for the nation.

Among the top-ten research proposals – along with compelling ideas to build economic prosperity by reforming EDH, improving the Cap-Haïtien port, and expanding mobile broadband access, and to reduce trauma deaths by training first responders – are six proposals that would make a big difference while the clock is ticking on a child's earliest development.

When a child is born, a clock starts ticking. Scientists have shown that half of a child's intelligence potential is developed by the age of four. Early development makes a huge difference to life-long wellbeing.

It is little surprise that distinguished economists who studied responses to Haitian challenges has focused attention on powerful investments that target children in infancy and in the womb.

The panel heard the research by World Health Organization economist Karin Stenberg and co-authors showing that improving access to emergency obstetric care to manage complications around birth would avert 505 maternal deaths per year. As has been outlined earlier, nearly 4,000 more newborns would survive each year, and 859 stillbirths would be prevented. Every gourde spent on this would generate benefits to society worth 16 gourdes.

Once a child is born, it is crucial to provide protection against illness. Ministry of Planning and External Cooperation (MPCE) economist Magdine Flore Rozier Baldé presented evidence to the panel on the benefits of lifting infant immunization coverage to 90% by 2020, and found that doing so would cost 2.4 billion gourdes over five years, immunize 864,000 additional children, and save more than 16,000 lives. Benefits are worth 32.3 billion gourdes, making it a phenomenal investment.

Increasing family planning access is another proposal the Eminent Panel declared one of the top priorities for Haiti. Doing so would cost 1,496 gourdes per woman, or 1,543 million gourdes annually to reach all of the women in Haiti who need this, according to Professor Hans-Peter

Kohler of the University of Pennsylvania. He found that family planning programs have a myriad of benefits: they reduce maternal and child mortality, improve child health, female education, women's general health, female labor-force participation and earnings.

In Haiti, the under-five mortality rate could be cut by as much as 70% through improved family planning access. Having fewer children means relatively more people of working age, making Haiti slightly more productive. Taking this into account, every gourde spent on expanding sexual reproductive health services would generate benefits worth 18 gourdes.

Early in a child's life, access to educational stimulation can create the conditions for success as an adult. Education economist Atonu Rabbani presented evidence to the eminent panel showing that two years of teacher-led play sessions that help with things like socialization would cost around 5,500 gourdes (US$79) per student per year. A famous, long-term research experiment in Jamaica gives good reason to believe that such a policy will lead to an increase of 35 percent in future earnings. Based on the compelling return on investment – 14 gourdes for every gourde spent – the eminent panel found that this should be a priority for Haiti.

Kesner Pharel concluded that, "Early childhood education can instill a love of learning that lasts a child's entire life."

And, powerfully, the panel found that improving nutrition is one of the most powerful investments that can be made in a young child's life. The distinguished economists considered research by Stephen Vosti of the University of California, Davis, and colleagues, on the merits of adding iron and folic acid to wheat flour when it is milled or bagged in Haiti. This is called "fortification", and can be adapted to add vital micronutrients to any staple food product.

Although this would improve folic acid and iron intake for everyone, it would have the biggest impacts for pregnant women and young children. Spending 331 million gourdes to fortify 95% of wheat flour will stop 140 neural tube defect deaths and more than 250,000 cases of anemia annually. This is relatively cheap, and has huge and lasting impacts worth 7.9 billion gourdes in financial terms. Raymond Magloire pointed out, "Wheat flour fortification is a very cheap intervention, involving cooperation between the government and Haitian industry to ensure that micronutrients are added at the mill. I find that there is a compelling case that fortifying a staple food product could make a significant difference to an important nutritional problem."

Similarly, Ketleen Florestal concluded that the proposal has "transformative" potential: "if carried out correctly in the Haitian context, this could improve the diets and health of many people and remove a significant disadvantage from a significant portion of the population."

Turning from early childhood to other policies, the top-ten priorities include training volunteers across Haiti to act as paramedics and first responders, which would have an annual cost of just 80 million gourdes, but would save around 700 lives every year. Each gourde would produce 16 gourdes of social good, according to Applied Economist at the Ministry of Public Health and Population R. Christina Daurisca.

As Raymond Magloire concluded, "The low cost of training first responders makes it a highly attractive health investment. In the absence of a Haitian ambulance network, it is eminently sensible to consider what we can achieve with trained volunteers."

The final two top-ten solutions relate to approaches to improving the nation's economy. Streamlining imports with an electronic port custom system was analyzed for the Cap-Haïtien Port; here it would reduce bureaucratic delays, strengthen border security, and reduce port costs, creating benefits worth 5.24 billion gourdes, according to research by Yvrose Guerrier, department head at the Ministry of Planning and External Cooperation. Every gourde spent would create 7 gourdes of benefits.

Creating the conditions for an autonomous, accountable and efficient electric utility was the panel's top recommendation.

(Ketleen Florestal recused herself from the ranking of proposals relating to the energy sector in order to avoid potential conflicts of interest.)

The proposal, studied by Juan Belt, Bahman Kashi, and Jay Mackinnon of Limestone Analytics, would cost 2.25 billion gourdes. Drawing lessons from reforms carried out in the Kabul Electricity Service Improvement Program and the authors' experience in working with the electricity sector in Haiti, they suggest a two-phase approach for the reform of the public utility, Electricité d'Haiti (EDH).

This would first see changes in the institutional and regulatory framework of the power sector, corporatizing and reforming of the governance structures of the 10 units of EDH, and establishing cost-reflective tariffs. The second phase, conditional on the success of the first phase, would include providing technical advisory and limited investment funds for continued improvement in service delivery and financial efficiency. This would reduce the EDH's current significant losses.

Belt and colleagues point out that even if one only looks at a reduction in the technical losses, the project will still pay off handsomely. They note that "even then, the project can easily recover its costs in multiples. The project can eliminate the need for $200 million in annual subsidies, which will unlock the potential for an array of investments in additional generation, distribution, and transmission capacity."

Kesner Pharel goes even further, noting that, "freeing up $200 million dollars per year means this money could be better spent on areas like health and education, to achieve a lot more for Haiti." He finds that "there are many infrastructure needs, but among them electricity reform is indispensable. Reform will be challenging, but it is vital."

There is also lots of theft of electricity – typically by corrupt middle-men. Reducing this theft and bringing better electricity to everyone in Haiti through reform of EDH will generate benefits to Haiti worth US$723 million (49 billion gourdes). Each gourde or dollar spent on this proposal would generate benefits worth 22 gourdes. Crucially, reforming EDH would remove one of the nation's most significant barriers to economic development.

The Eminent Panel's top-ten ranked priorities, covering health, immunization, infrastructure and education, together represent a portfolio of investment options which would generate incredible returns for Haiti.

It is hugely promising that, after being presented with these findings, Haitian President Jovenel Moïse undertook to require wheat to be fortified with vital micronutrients within one year. This is a vital action that could save many, many lives.

It is our hope that this, and actions motivated by the data presented in this book, will result in considerable benefits for Haiti, for many years to come.

EMINENT PANEL PRIORITIZATION

The Eminent Panel comprises Ketleen Florestal who has worked since 2010 at the World Bank Group as an Advisor to the Executive Director for Haiti; Dr. Kesner Pharel, a prominent economist playing a central role in the dissemination and sensitization of economic issues, especially matters concerning public finance, via his weekly commentary on RadioTele Metropole and innumerable speaking engagements; Philomé Joseph Raymond Magloire, former governor of the Central Bank (BRH), who specializes in finance and economics; Dr. Vernon L. Smith, who was awarded the Nobel Prize in Economic Sciences in 2002 for his groundbreaking work in experimental economics.

The panel examined the proposals in detail. Each proposal was discussed with its principal author. The panel was informed by Sector Expert Review papers, and by their own critical appraisals and discussions on assumptions and methodology.

In ordering the proposals, the Eminent Panel was guided predominantly by consideration of social, economic and environmental costs and benefits.

The Eminent Panel acknowledged the difficulties that cost-benefit analysis must overcome, both in principle and as a practical matter, but agreed that the cost-benefit approach was an indispensable organizing method. Each Eminent Panel member assigned his or her own ranking to proposals. The Eminent Panel's ranking was calculated by taking the median of individual rankings. The Eminent Panel jointly endorses the median ordering as representing their agreed view.

The Eminent Panel considers and prioritizes specific proposals to respond to challenges. This is different from ranking the challenges themselves. A low ranking of a proposal does not mean that the problem it addresses should be considered unimportant.

The ranking of certain proposals including national legal aid system, domestic violence helpline and digitization of government services were affected by factors including the availability of data, and may have been given a lower ranking among other reasons due to concerns that the proposals would not adequately resolve important aspects of the challenges they were designed to address.

However, the Eminent Panel stresses the importance of reducing domestic violence, resolving legal system shortcomings, and improving government services.

Regarding the challenge of domestic violence, the Eminent Panel specifically notes the beneficial effect that higher-ranked proposals are likely to have on this challenge, through financial empowerment of girls and women. Such effects were taken into consideration.

The Eminent Panel also notes the importance of improving wages, particularly for women, as well as the registration of birth and provision of identity documents. It recommends that a broad range of measures be studied, including improvements to the existing system, and that the electronic registration be not considered in isolation.

Careful attention should be paid to the institutional and financial arrangements for implementing these proposals, such as in the case of crop transport truck systems.

In setting priorities, the Eminent Panel took into account the strengths and weaknesses of the specific cost-benefit appraisals under review, and gave weight both to the institutional preconditions for success and to the demands of ethical or humanitarian importance.

Based on the costs and benefits of the solutions and their own assessment, the panel ranked the proposals, in descending order of desirability, as follows:

Rank	Proposal
1	reform electricity utility
2	wheat flour micronutrient fortification
3	early childhood stimulation
4	train first responders
5	immunization for children 0-1
6	maternal and newborn health
7	access to contraception
8	skilled assistance at delivery
9	expand mobile broadband
10	electronic port custom system

Rank	Proposal
11	electronic registration of birth certificate
12	calcium and micronutrients in pregnancy
13	micronutrient powder ½-2-year olds
14	girls' retention in school
15	local child nutrition formula RUTF
16	teaching children at the right level
17	standard child nutrition formula RUTF
18	decentralized government
19	distribution grid extension and upgrade
20	digitize government processes
21	shelters for women and children
22	national power transmission grid
23	train teachers
24	manage childhood illnesses
25	flood early warning system
26	cholera 1 dose school vaccination
27	conditional cash transfers secondary school
28	mobile school clinics
29	rural community health centers
30	flood early warning system and shelters
31	rural borehole and handpump
32	vocational training
33	better agroforestry
34	cholera 1 dose mass vaccination
35	digitize land records
36	rural community led total sanitation
37	performance pay in public service
38	diabetes treatment for children
39	expand urban ambulance network
40	expand graduation program
41	road Gonaives to P-d-P
42	e-voting
43	crop transport truck system
44	private school subsidies
45	HIV test and treatment
46	gas power ACC
47	cholera 2 dose mass vaccination
48	promote improved cookstoves
49	civic education for youth
50	clinics at each school
51	teach in creole

Rank	Proposal
52	national legal aid system
53	biogas scale-up
54	establish national ambulance network
55	coal power
56	national patrol force
57	free school uniforms
58	off-grid hydro for village
59	hypertension campaign and full treatment
60	off-grid diesel for village
61	hydro power
62	expand microcredit program
63	wind power
64	introduce crop insurance
65	switch charcoal cookstoves to gas
66	packaging and conservation center
67	domestic violence helpline
68	subsidize fertilizer for rice
69	urban container based sanitation
70	solar photovoltaic power
71	bridge Les Anglais
72	local content procurement
73	agricultural R&D
74	pit latrines in urban areas
75	diesel, solar and battery for village
76	improved and intensified rice production
77	switch wood cookstoves to gas
78	prevent teen dating violence
79	solar reflective power
80	vaccinate girls against cervical cancer
81	carbon pricing infrastructure
82	20% rice tariff for ten years
83	increase public service pay 10%
84	increase domestic worker wages*
85	paid paternity leave

The Eminent Panel stresses the importance of increasing wages, especially for women, but the specific proposal considered was not sufficiently clear on the net benefits for the target group. Eminent Panel member Ketleen Florestal recused herself from the ranking of proposals relating to the energy sector in order to avoid potential conflicts of interest.

Made in the USA
Middletown, DE
17 June 2020